CAN I GO HOME WITH YOU?

CAN I GO HOME WITH YOU?

CHLOE'S STORY OF TRAUMA, DISRUPTED ATTACHMENT, AND PSYCHOTROPIC MEDICATION

THE ORP LIBRARY

WRITTEN BY

JEFF KRUKAR, PH.D.
KATIE GUTIERREZ
CHELSEA McCUTCHIN

WITH

NICOLETTE WEISENSEL, M.D.
JAMES G. BALESTRIERI

rtc Publishing

Copyright © 2016

WRITERS OF THE ROUND TABLE PRESS
PO BOX 511
HIGHLAND PARK, IL 60035

Publisher	COREY MICHAEL BLAKE
Executive Editor	KATIE GUTIERREZ
Lead Writer	CHELSEA MCCUTCHIN
President	KRISTIN WESTBERG
Facts Keeper	MIKE WINICOUR
Cover Design	ANALEE PAZ
Interior Design and Layout	SUNNY DIMARTINO, CHRISTY BUI
Proofreading	JONATHAN HIERHOLZER
Last Looks	CHRISTIAN PANNECK
Digital Book Conversion	SUNNY DIMARTINO
Digital Publishing	SUNNY DIMARTINO

Printed in the United States of America
First Edition: May 2016
10 9 8 7 6 5 4 3 2 1

Library of Congress Cataloging-in-Publication Data
Krukar, Jeff
Can I go home with you?: chloe's story of trauma,
disrupted attachment, and psychotropic medication /
Jeff Krukar, Katie Gutierrez, and Chelsea McCutchin
with Nicolette Weisensel and James G. Balestrieri.—1st ed. p. cm.
Print ISBN: 978-1-939418-81-4   Digital ISBN: 978-1-939418-82-1
Library of Congress Control Number: 2016938449
Number 15 in the series: The ORP Library
The ORP Library: Can I Go Home with You?

RTC Publishing is an imprint of Writers of the Round Table, Inc.
Writers of the Round Table Press and the RTC Publishing logo
are trademarks of Writers of the Round Table, Inc.

CONTENTS

INTRODUCTION

Today, according to the U.S. Department of Health and Human Services, more than 5.5 million children—or eight percent of kids—in the U.S. have some form of disability. Whether the problem is physical, behavioral, or emotional, these children struggle to communicate, learn, and relate to others. While there is no longer *segregation* in the same sense as there was in the 1950s, what remains the same is the struggle. Even with all of our resources and technology, parents of children with disabilities fight battles every day to find the help and education their children need.

I have led Oconomowoc Residential Programs (ORP) for over thirty years. We're a family of companies offering specialized services and care for children, adolescents, and adults with disabilities. Too often, when parents of children with disabilities try to find funding for programs like ours, they are bombarded by red tape, conflicting information, or no information at all, so they struggle blindly for years to secure an appropriate education. Meanwhile, home life, and the child's wellbeing, suffers. In cases when parents and caretakers have exhausted their options—and their hope—ORP is here to help. We felt it was time to offer parents a new, unexpected tool to fight back: stories that educate, empower, and inspire.

The original idea was to create a library of comic books that could empower families with information to reclaim their rights. We wanted to give parents and caretakers the information they need to advocate for themselves, as well as provide educators and therapists with a therapeutic tool. And, of course, we wanted to reach the children—to offer them a visual representation of their journey that would show that they aren't alone, nor are they wrong or "bad" for their differences. What we found in the process of writing original stories for the comics is that these journeys are too long, too complex, to be contained within a standard comic. So what we are now creating is an ORP library of disabilities books—traditional books geared toward parents, caretakers, educators, and therapists, *and* comic books portraying the world through the eyes of children with disabilities. Both styles of books share what we have learned while advocating for families over the years while also honestly highlighting their emotional journeys. We're creating communication devices that anyone can read to understand complex disabilities in a new way.

In an ideal situation, these books will be used therapeutically, to communicate the message, and to help support the work ORP and companies like ours are doing. The industry has changed dramatically and is not likely to turn around any time soon—certainly not without more people being aware of families' struggles. We have an opportunity to put a face to the conversation, reach out to families, and start that dialogue.

Caring for children with disabilities consumes your life. We know that. And we want you to realize, through these stories, that you are not alone. We can help.

Sincerely,
Jim Balestrieri
CEO, Oconomowoc Residential Programs
www.orplibrary.com

A NOTE ABOUT THIS BOOK

Psychotropic medications are prescribed for the treatment of psychiatric disorders and specifically to improve a patient's emotional and behavioral health. In children and adolescents, just as in adults, lack of appropriate treatment can result in both short-term and long-term consequences.

Since the mid to late 1990s, there has been a significant increase in the understanding of childhood psychiatric disorders and a developing evidence base to support psychotropic medication and other nonmedication treatments for children with these disorders. Unfortunately, despite these advances, the majority of children and adolescents do not receive appropriate evaluations and treatment.

Changes in the U.S. mental health system over the last 20 years have resulted in a shortage of child and adolescent psychiatrists, increasingly limited insurance coverage for inpatient and residential treatment, and limited outpatient alternatives to support what many believe is an increased need for services. The front lines of the mental health services battle now squarely reside in the office of the primary care provider. These physicians now furnish over half of the mental health treatment in the U.S. and are believed to prescribe the majority of psychotropic medications used by children and adolescents (Bazelton Center). While each primary care provider's education and experience varies, most are unlikely to have the appropriate resources to treat youth who have a complicated set of challenges.

Unfortunately, there has also been an insufficient number of psychotropic medication trials with children and adolescents. This has left few psychotropic medications that are Food and Drug Administration (FDA) approved for use in youth. As a result, many psychotropic medications prescribed for this age group are administered "off label"—that is, not FDA approved for use in children and adolescents for certain disorders or age ranges. In clinical practice, however, the majority of "off label" psychotropic medications do appear to be beneficial and safe in youth.

Psychotropic medications are only one component of a comprehensive biopsychosocial treatment plan, which must be a collaborative team effort and include other components in addition to medication. The term *biopsychosocial* recognizes the three domains that impact a youth's emotional and behavioral well-being:

1. *Bio* refers to "biological," and includes physical health and genetic factors. Psychotropic medications affect biological factors by altering the levels of chemicals in the brain that help to regulate the activity of neurons (brain cells) that determine emotions, mood, and behavior.

2. *Psycho* refers to psychological factors in the youth that contribute to emotional and behavioral functioning, including feelings and thoughts, goals, and understanding of self and environment.

3. *Social* refers to the environmental factors that influence a youth's functioning, such as family circumstances and relationships and other resources in the community, including those provided by human service agencies and natural supports. Within the social domain, it is particularly important to obtain the evaluation of history of trauma and disrupted attachments.

Health professionals, families, advocates, and human service providers must carefully assess the risks and benefits of using psychotropic medications in children and adolescents. Readers are encouraged to educate themselves appropriately depending on their individual situation, and to be careful to obtain information from reputable sources. An appendix is located at the end of this book with resources to consider using.

The child depicted in the following story struggles with significant emotional and behavioral difficulties. You may note similarities to your own experiences or those of a loved one, student, or patient. If so, this book is meant to provide a roadmap, of sorts. It is our hope that the education it provides will help you navigate the complex journey experienced by those whose worlds intersect with the use of psychotropic medications.

Jim Balestrieri
CEO, Oconomowoc Residential Programs

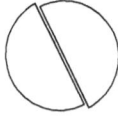

CHAPTER 1

It was nine p.m. when Tamara emerged from the shower, surprised to hear the home phone ringing. Rarely did they get calls on the home line, especially this late. She wrapped herself in a towel and rushed to the foyer, dripping a path along the tile.

"Hello?" she answered, not recognizing the number on her caller ID.

"Mrs. Ramsey?" It was a woman's voice, firm and professional. "This is Stacy Kleber, with county social services."

Tamara sank onto the cedar chest where she and her husband, Darryl, stored their winter coats during the summer. Her heart jumped with recognition: this was about their niece, Chloe. It had to be.

"Yes, hi, Stacy," Tamara said. "How can I help you?"

"Is your husband available?" Stacy asked.

"No, I'm sorry, he's not home yet." Tamara paused before asking again, "Can I help with something?"

The line was quiet a second too long. Tamara closed her eyes. "Is it Chloe? Is she okay?"

"Chloe is fine," Stacy said.

"Oh, thank God."

"But Mrs. Ramsey, I'm sorry to inform you that your sister-in-law, Jasmine Ramsey, has passed away." Stacy's calm voice wavered with sympathy. "As your husband is listed as her next of kin, we need him to come to the coroner's office and make the identification."

"Oh, no. What happened? What about Chloe?" Tamara asked, her niece's dark eyes flashing across her mind.

Tamara and Darryl had been fighting for custody of Chloe since she was eighteen months old. Jasmine had long struggled with drug addiction. It had started with party drugs—coke and ecstasy—before the terrifying transition to heroin. Darryl's mother had cared for the baby from when she was six months old until about nine months old. When Beticia had suddenly passed away from a massive stroke, Chloe returned to live with Jasmine. But Jasmine was ill-equipped to be a mother. She wore noise cancellation headphones to mute Chloe's crying, left her in a home daycare run by one older woman with seven other charges, and shuffled her from one house party to another on weekends. Darryl and Tamara lived with a constant, horrified sense of foreboding, convinced that at some point, something terrible would happen: Jasmine would leave Chloe in the car while she ran a "quick" errand, or there would be an accident, or both Jasmine and Chloe would be at the wrong place at the wrong time. They begged Jasmine to let them care for Chloe while she went to rehab, but Jasmine refused. Finally, Darryl and Tamara had contacted the department of child and family services. Chloe had been removed from Jasmine at eighteen months, but she was later returned to her mother's "care." The court system had given Jasmine multiple chances to change through required counseling and parenting classes. Few were the ones Jasmine attended. While foster care was strongly considered, the county never initiated the process.

"Chloe is with me," Stacy said. "Since she was in her mother's custody at the time of her death, she is officially a ward of the state."

"Can we come get her? You know we've been trying to get custody of her?" Tamara's voice hitched, and she took a deep breath, releasing it slowly, to calm her heart rate. When Darryl walked in from the garage, he drew his brows together quizzically, silently asking who was on the phone. Tamara extended a hand toward him, and he walked toward her.

"Yes," Stacy said. "We can meet you at the police station. I am so sorry for your loss."

"Thank you. We'll be there as soon as we can." Tamara hung up the phone and looked up at Darryl. His deep brown eyes were hooded with the overtime he'd been putting in lately, and his cheeks were dark with what they called his one o'clock shadow; by now, evidence of Darryl's morning shave had all but disappeared. Tamara stood and placed a hand on his forearm. The only way to say it was to say it.

"Baby. Jasmine's gone."

Darryl shook his head. "Of course she is," he said, his voice tight. "And let me guess, Chloe will be in a foster home somewhere until they can find her worthless mother?"

"No, honey." Tamara paused, biting her lip. "Jasmine is *gone*. She passed away."

Jasmine was Darryl's younger sister, and while the two had never been close, she was the only blood relative Darryl had left. Their father had died when he and Jasmine were children. While their mother had done the best she could, Jasmine had never grown out of the

3

rebellion she entered after her father's death. Now, at hearing the news, Darryl felt oddly startled. Though why should he be? This was the road Jasmine had picked, as much as she loved to play the victim; like he and his mother had always told her, death or jail were the only places this road led. Inexplicably, he was angry with himself for being surprised at the news, even for a moment. He gripped on to the anger.

"I knew this would happen," he said. "I told her. I told her I'd be identifying her body one day."

Jasmine wasn't a good mother, or even a good person, most of the time. She'd stolen from Darryl and their mother, and she'd never taken care of her child but done her best to ensure that Darryl and the "uppity bitch" he'd married never got custody of her. But she was his sister. And a fissure in his chest, like the crackling of ice, registered the loss.

Tamara's eyes had brightened with tears, but she blinked them back and reached for his hand. He appreciated that about his wife, that she could set her own feelings aside to be there for him. But he was restless, all coiled energy. He stood up, sliding his hand from hers, before she could say a word to comfort him.

"What do we need to do?" Darryl asked.

Tamara held her towel, just for something to do with her hands. "We need to go to the police station. Stacy, the social worker, is going to meet us there with Chloe. I'm sorry, Darryl—they do need you to identify her."

"You ought to get dressed," Darryl said, walking to the bedroom. For a moment, Tamara felt a tremble of knowing: Darryl was going to try not to feel this. He was going to avoid and ignore his emotions. He was going to shut her out. It had happened after his mother died, and it would happen again now, only now they would have Chloe.

Tamara shook off her thoughts. There was no right way to respond to this, she reminded herself as she followed Darryl and pulled on the pair of jeans and t-shirt she had worn earlier that day. She slid her feet into a pair of flip-flops, and they rode in silence to the police station.

When they arrived, Darryl, in a daze, was led off by a detective while Tamara was taken to an interview room. The room smelled like coffee and a recent paint job.

Chloe was sitting in a chair pulled close to a woman with wavy brown hair tossed into a messy bun. The woman's wire-rimmed glasses were smudged with fingerprints. Chloe was leaning into her, shoulder to shoulder, stroking the woman's hand. "Can we go now?" she was asking. "Can I go home with you?"

The level of familiarity Chloe was showing to the woman, presumably Stacy, was startling. But it at least suggested that Stacy had been an active participant in Chloe's care, which was reassuring.

"Hi, baby!" Tamara consciously kept her voice light, but her affection for Chloe wasn't feigned. She loved this child. "And you must be Stacy," she said.

"It's nice to meet you, Mrs. Ramsey, though again, I'm terribly sorry for the circumstances." Stacy turned to Chloe. "Chloe, do you see your auntie?" she cooed.

Chloe looked up. "Hi, Tam," she said, before directing her attention back to Stacy. "So? Can we go? I like you. Don't you like me? I'll be good."

Stacy gave Tamara a stiff smile. "Of course I like you," she said to Chloe. "But your aunt is here to take you home to *her* house. Won't that be nice?"

5

Chloe looked between the two women, and Tamara knelt so that she was eye to eye with the child. "Hey, baby girl. I'm happy to see you. Do you want to come to our house?" she asked gingerly.

Chloe's face was impassive. Then she smiled and reached out to touch the stiff ends of Tamara's braids. "Okay," she said. "Can Stacy come, too?"

"I'm afraid not tonight," Tamara said. "Honey, I need to talk to Stacy for a minute. We're going to be right outside, okay? Here." She reached inside her purse and pulled out her phone, clicking to the game she'd downloaded for Chloe the last time they'd visited. "Why don't you play your game while Stacy and I have a little talk?"

Chloe shrugged, and her too-large shirt slipped, revealing the top of a filthy nightgown. She took the phone and didn't look up as Tamara and Stacy left the room.

Outside, Tamara looked at Stacy. "Chloe seems very attached to you," she remarked.

Stacy gave a small, troubled smile. "Yes," she said. "She was like this immediately, which is a little disconcerting since it's the first time we've met."

Tamara blinked. "Really? I just assumed . . ."

"No. I've only been her caseworker for a week, and my first home visit wasn't scheduled for another two," Stacy said.

Tamara forced herself to smile. She felt a flicker of . . . what? Jealousy, she realized, that Chloe seemed more taken by a stranger than by her own aunt. "Well, she's probably learned to be a good judge of character," Tamara said. "Listen, Stacy, we would like for Chloe to stay with us for good. We've been trying to get her mother to agree for years."

"I know," Stacy said. "I've read her file."

"What are the next steps to make that happen?"

"Well, Chloe needs to be evaluated by a pediatrician. I have her medical records, and from what I can gather, the last time she went to the doctor was for her three-year-old well-child exam."

"A full year ago?" Tamara asked, indignant. "What else?"

"Tamara, I called the police this afternoon because I wasn't able to get in touch with Jasmine for her monthly check-in. She's only had Chloe back this time for three weeks, and it's always a red flag when we're unable to make contact. The police were going to check it out tomorrow, but they received a 911 call from the address. When they got there, the door was open, the house was trashed, and Jasmine was on the couch, already gone. We're assuming that whoever she was using with left when they realized that Jasmine wasn't just passed out, but they did put in the emergency call first."

Tamara's anger at Jasmine reached around the horrified sadness. "And Chloe?" she asked, hardly wanting to know the answer.

Stacy nodded. "Chloe was hiding behind Jasmine's bed when the police found her. We have no idea what she's seen or experienced in the past few weeks—even months, if we're being honest. When I arrived, she was wearing a soiled diaper. I don't even want to hazard a guess on the last time she was changed, and of course she's four years old; she should be potty trained by now. I brought a car seat—which I can let you use tonight—along with diapers, wipes, and a change of clothes. The clothes are size 3T, but as you can see, they're hanging off her. She looks malnourished, and I saw some nasty sores on her bottom." Stacy paused, as though trying to keep her tone professional. "It's pretty obvious that she hasn't been bathed for a few days, and I took her to a drive-thru on the way to the police station—she ate all of her kid's meal and half of my chicken nuggets, so she was clearly hungry. I wish I had been assigned to her earlier . . . There are just so many cases."

The information was heart wrenching, too much so to truly consider. Tamara packed it away and tried to stay in the present. "Well, now we have her, she's safe, and that's all that matters. Do I need to take her to the hospital tonight?"

Stacy nodded. "Yes. The ER will see her. The police have already informed them that you're arriving. I've forwarded all of Chloe's medical history that I have access to."

The interview room door opened a crack, and Chloe's little nose poked out.

"Come here, baby," Tamara said, once again squatting to embrace the child on her level. Chloe accepted Tamara's hug, but her arms hung limply by her sides. Just then, Darryl came down the hallway, his eyes red-rimmed. He met Tamara and Chloe where they stood, low to the ground, and wrapped his arms around them both. For a long moment he just held them, appreciating their warmth.

When they rose, Tamara told Darryl in her happiest voice that they were going to the doctor with Chloe. If he would drop them off, he could go get some clean clothes and diapers at the twenty-four-hour superstore. Or she'd be happy to trade and go to the store while he stayed with Chloe at the doctor. He told Tamara that he didn't mind doing some shopping for his favorite little girl.

"Can Stacy come?" Chloe asked again. She peered up at the three adults, wrapping her arms around Stacy's leg. "I want her to come. I love her!"

Darryl gave Tamara a baffled look. "Uh, no, Chloe. Maybe Stacy can come visit later in the week. Tonight it will be just you, Tam, and me."

Color rose to Chloe's cheeks as she clung more tightly to Stacy. She pressed her cheek against the social worker's jeans. "No!" she yelled. "I want Stacy!"

Stacy's back was stiff, and her arms hung straight at her sides. She forced a smile. "Chloe, honey, I'll be seeing you later. You need to go with your family tonight."

"They're not my family. I don't have a family!" Chloe's voice had become petulant, defiant. "I had a mom, but she's dead now."

The words struck Darryl like a fist in his solar plexus. Already hating himself for what he was about to do, he told Tamara, "I can't deal with this. I'll be in the car."

Tamara opened her mouth to protest, but it was too late: Darryl was walking away, leaving her to pry Chloe from the social worker on her own.

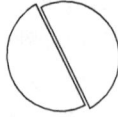

CHAPTER 2

Two months later, Tamara smiled at the guest room that she and Darryl had transformed into a bedroom fit for a princess. They'd collected pink butterfly curtains and sheets, carefully painted a dresser and nightstand, and filled a toy box with Barbies, puzzles, and dancing fairies. While this wasn't how she'd anticipated becoming a mother, she was just thrilled to have her newly adopted daughter home where she belonged.

The process had been quick: while Jasmine hadn't created a will, a judge ruled favorably that Chloe should be adopted by Darryl and Tamara. In addition to being next of kin, which didn't automatically guarantee such a ruling, their years of advocating for Chloe had been carefully documented. After the hearing, Stacy had given Tamara a heartfelt hug. "This is what we hope for," she'd said, "that the children in our system will find good, loving homes. It doesn't always work out that way. I'm glad it has for Chloe."

The time since that first night at the police station hadn't been easy. Tamara cringed when she remembered Chloe screaming, begging for Stacy to come with them. She'd felt as though she were kidnapping her own niece, right in the cynical gaze of surrounding police officers. But once they were in the car, Chloe had quieted instantly. Tamara could almost convince herself that she'd imagined the tantrum.

"I'm sorry," Darryl had said quietly, resting a hand on Tamara's thigh. "I just couldn't deal with everything right then." Tamara had nodded. She understood.

Under FMLA, Tamara had taken leave from work to bond with Chloe and get her settled. The transition had been bittersweet. While Tamara and Darryl had relished preparing Chloe's room, Chloe didn't seem to know what to do with any of the toys. It was as though she couldn't distinguish between a doll and a branch. The closest she came to playing was to sit beside her Barbies, who were often half naked and "sleeping."

There were other things, too—things that seemed *off* to Tamara but that she lacked the language to fully articulate. There was the way Chloe had acted with Stacy, for example. It wasn't the last time she would become overly attached to someone she just met. "She's very friendly," Tamara would say apologetically at the grocery store or the mall, taking Chloe firmly by the hand and leading her away, wailing, from her new "friend." Tamara wasn't sure what to make of this. Was it entirely abnormal behavior? Or did it make a kind of sense, considering Chloe's background, that she would gravitate toward any adult who felt safe or showed her even a tiny kindness—a smile, a pat on the head? Investigating took the backburner, at least for a while, to Chloe's more immediate medical needs.

Chloe needed extensive nutritional supplementation, and the nasty sores on her bottom had turned out to be methicillin-resistant Staphylococcus aureus (MSRA).

The doctor speculated that Chloe was living in deeply unsanitary conditions, perhaps going hours without being changed or days without being bathed. He'd given her a round of antibiotics, but when the MSRA was unresponsive, he'd had to drain some of the abscesses. Afterward, Chloe screamed in pain. Tamara's internal mantra, as she tried to comfort Chloe, became *Damn you, Jasmine.*

For his part, Darryl rarely talked about his sister. He had gone to her place to collect anything worth keeping—photo albums, their mother's cross necklace (which she had given to Jasmine to keep her safe)—and then hired a cleaning company to dispose of the rest. Anytime Tamara tried asking Darryl how he was feeling, he shook his head. "Not now," he would say. After a while, Tamara stopped asking. Darryl buried himself in work, coming home at eight or nine at night, barely masking his irritation that there was no dinner waiting. Tamara was always apologetic and frazzled, explaining how she'd intended to cook for the two of them after Chloe was in bed, but Chloe was impossible to put down. Darryl would pour a large bowl of cereal and take it to their bedroom, where he usually fell asleep before finishing it. Sometimes, as Tamara coaxed him up and helped him out of his slacks and wrinkled shirt, she felt she was caring for two children.

As Tamara would have to return to work in two weeks, she'd been searching for a daycare center that could be sensitive to Chloe's needs. From what Tamara could discern, although Chloe was four, she had poorly developed academic pre-readiness skills. After touring three daycare centers, she was most impressed with the one that would work with Chloe on basic shapes, letters, numbers, and color recognition, as well as basic hygiene, potty training, and socialization skills. Tamara and Darryl had met the teacher, Bianca, and immediately felt a sense of relief: she was a certified special education teacher who had experience working with students like Chloe.

After talking it over, they decided to enroll Chloe later that day. In the meantime, Tamara thought she would tidy Chloe's room. As Chloe looked at a puzzle on the pink tulip rug in the center of her room, Tamara bent behind the toy box to pick up a few fallen stuffed animals.

"Tam! No!" Chloe cried.

"What is it, baby?" Tamara asked. "I'm just picking up. Do you want to help?" Tamara picked up a glittery unicorn and tossed it into the toy box. "See? I'm not taking anything away."

Chloe continued to wail, and when Tamara looked back down at the small pile of stuffed animals, she saw why: behind her toy box, Chloe had stashed two sleeves of saltine crackers, a jar of peanut butter, three packs of fruit snacks, and six juice boxes. As Tamara pulled out the food, bewildered, Chloe collapsed to the floor.

"Sweetheart, why are you so upset?" Tamara asked, dropping beside the little girl.

"Don't take my food, Tam!" Chloe's eyes were desperate. "I need it! Give it back!"

"Chloe, we'll get roaches and ants and rats in here if we keep our food out. We need to store it in the kitchen, where we can keep it clean." Tamara had no idea how to comfort her child, who was screaming as if she were being tortured. Tamara stood to take the food into the other room, but as soon as she hit the hallway, she heard the rip of Velcro. Turning back around, she saw that Chloe had removed her diaper and was squatting on the floor, her face red with effort.

"Chloe!" she exclaimed, dropping the food and rushing to the child. "We don't do that! When we have to go poo poo, we use the potty!" Tamara tried to pull Chloe's arm to encourage her to follow her to the bathroom, but Chloe bucked, making Tamara lose her grip as Chloe tumbled back into her own excrement. The child wailed as she hit the ground, but just as quickly she stood, her eyes defiant as she grabbed her discarded diaper and hurled it at Tamara. Chloe's aim and strength were poor, so the diaper hit the floor a foot away from Tamara's ankle. At a loss, Tamara stepped over it to pull Chloe up by the armpits and carry her to the bathtub.

Chloe didn't calm, despite the warm water and lavender soap. "No bath, no bath!" she screamed, thrashing and slipping despite the grippy duck decals Tamara had stuck on the bathtub floor. Tamara winced when Chloe's knee hit the porcelain, intensifying the pitch of her wailing. Once she was clean, and still screaming, Tamara returned her to the bedroom, where she struggled to fit her in a diaper before just grabbing the soiled rug and walking out of the room.

After dropping the rug in the laundry room, Tamara returned to stand in the doorway of Chloe's bedroom. She didn't know what to do for this little girl, who was beside herself with emotion she couldn't express and Tamara couldn't begin to interpret. The veins throbbed at Tamara's temples, but she couldn't bear to leave Chloe alone—even though Tamara doubted her daughter would notice.

Tamara had always felt a cloud of resentment for those mothers who complained about how difficult parenting was as she, Tamara, disappointedly bought tampons month after month, as she tracked and charted and temped, prayed and cried and even made an offer at an altar devoted to Marie Laveau in New Orleans on vacation. But now, staring at a child she couldn't seem to reach, she understood.

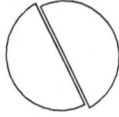

CHAPTER 3

"As you can see, Chloe really enjoys art," Bianca said, flipping her long dark hair over her shoulder as she displayed four drawings the little girl had created. "She's also come a long way with toilet training and general daily living, as well as self-care skills like washing her hands and blowing her nose. However, I have real concerns about sending her to kindergarten in the fall—she's just really behind the other kids socially and emotionally."

Tamara and Darryl looked at each other, both concerned by Bianca's assessment and half-relieved that their own worries weren't unfounded. Chloe had lived with them for nine months and been enrolled at her school for nearly seven. Bianca was now having parent conferences to discuss progress and kindergarten readiness. The three of them sat at a round table with chairs that were slightly too high, making Darryl, in particular, look like a giant looming over the table.

"You both know how much I care about Chloe," Bianca said. "However, we're unable to conduct our class without a significant disruption from her. Every morning at circle time, when I have the students sit 'crisscross applesauce' with their hands in their laps, Chloe wanders off through the centers. During free choice time, Chloe typically argues with other children because she doesn't understand their games. The students love their friend Chloe, but there seems to be a social gap, and she can leave them . . . frustrated." Gently, Bianca continued, "In my opinion, Chloe is struggling to fit in socially with the other kids and would benefit from another year in preschool before moving on to kindergarten."

Tamara nodded. She and Darryl had anticipated and even discussed this—and of course, it wasn't the first time they'd heard of Chloe's behavior in the classroom—but now Tamara was surprised by the blend of sadness and protectiveness she felt for her little girl. She sighed.

"We all know that Chloe had a rough start in life, so if another year of preschool will help better prepare her, then so be it. Actually, Bianca," Tamara added, "we have a question for you." Tamara looked over at Darryl, who nodded. "Whenever we see a new student at the school, there are typically a few days, if not weeks, of clinging to the parents and crying to go home. Chloe has never done that—not here, not anywhere. She's never afraid of being left alone, and she doesn't express any caution toward strangers—I mean, *none*. How unusual is that?"

Bianca was quiet for a moment, as if choosing her words carefully. "Every child develops at a different pace and in different ways. You can't base your expectations of your child on the actions of another."

"Bianca, you don't have to be PC with us," Tamara said. "I know that beyond this classroom, this is your area of expertise. Please tell us. What could be going on with our daughter? We've tried our hardest to help her adjust. She's still so young, but it's clear to us that something isn't right. What could it be?"

Bianca looked at them thoughtfully and then appeared to make up her mind. "Well, I'm not a psychologist, so the whole area of diagnosis is something I can't touch, but I do see her struggling with inattention and hyperactivity. And, yes, I have noticed that she's extremely friendly and trusting toward new adults, which could be . . . problematic. I'll be honest—an evaluation by a licensed child psychologist might be something to think about."

"A psychologist?" Tamara repeated, looking between Bianca and Darryl. "But she's so young. What could a psychologist possibly even diagnose at this age?"

A *child psychologist* is an individual with a doctoral degree (Ph.D.), licensed by individual states to practice psychology. He or she can provide psychological testing and evaluations, treat emotional and behavioral problems and mental disorders, and provide a variety of psychotherapeutic techniques. Psychologists are not able to prescribe psychotropic medications.

Tamara wasn't sure what she'd expected from her line of questioning, but now she felt defensive: surely with everything Chloe had been through, and her youthful inability to express her feelings, unusual behavior was to be expected. Even as the arguments formed in her mind, Tamara knew she was grasping. The truth was, she didn't have a reference point, and she was terrified to admit the possibility that what was underlying Chloe's odd self-sufficiency and her sometimes-aggression was something beyond an easy repair. It wasn't fair—not to Tamara and Darryl, who'd wanted Chloe for so long, or to Chloe herself, the girl with the long, curled eyelashes, skin as rich and beautiful as café au lait, and tight curls that were beginning to grow thick and velvety with Chloe's improved nutrition and stable lifestyle.

"I'm only trying to make some suggestions, Tamara," Bianca said reassuringly. "These are my thoughts as her teacher, but as her parents, you know her best."

"No, you're right," Darryl said, diffusing the tension. "Thank you for everything. I think we're in agreement that Chloe will spend another year with you." He stood, and the women followed suit.

In the car, Darryl tried to be delicate when he brought up Bianca's suggestion. He recognized that his wife's reaction was only masking her fear. "Tamara, I don't think it could hurt anything if we just had her evaluated. It's the same as taking her to the pediatrician and having her MRSA checked out. Had we just assumed it was a terrible diaper rash, she could have had far more serious problems than a few scars and some rounds of heavy-duty antibiotics. I think that catching whatever might be different about Chloe soon, and learning how to work with her, will help all of us—especially her."

Tamara stared out the window while her husband spoke. She heard every word, and each cut through the already tender spot in her heart that knew something wasn't right about Chloe. "She's been through a lot," Tamara said. "She's also made a lot of adjustments in the past year. Sure, they've all been positive, but they were substantial. She just needs an extra year with Bianca." Her voice was heavy with guilt as she tried to convince herself that what she said was true.

The next week, Tamara noticed that Chloe's healthy appetite was starting to catch up with her: the 3T clothes that she'd just grown into were too short around the ankles and too tight around her belly. Delighted, Tamara planned a girls' trip to the mall on Saturday afternoon.

Shopping with her mother had been Tamara's favorite thing to do when she was small, and she'd always day-dreamed about shopping with her own daughter some-day. In the department store, Tamara got Chloe situated on a bench while she turned to find her daughter's size in several different shoes. When she turned around with the shoeboxes in hand, Chloe was gone.

"Chloe?" Tamara dropped the shoeboxes and rushed around the corner. "Chloe!" Panicked, Tamara made her way to the checkout desk.

"I—I've lost my daughter," Tamara stammered to the teenager behind the register. "I need your help."

The girl blinked, startled from something she'd been laughing at on her phone. "Oh, yeah. Don't worry. This happens a lot, but we always find them." The girl put her hand on the phone. "What's she wearing?"

"I—she has on a green shirt. Sequins around the col-lar. A pink skirt with tulle. Sneakers. Her name is Chloe."

The girl entered an extension on her phone. "Yeah, hi," she said. "I have a lady here who's—" She paused, then laughed. "Okay, I'll send her over." To Tamara, she said, "She's in customer service. She ran right into our security guard. See? Everything's fine."

Tamara gave the girl a queasy smile and walked with determination to the customer service desk, where a grandmotherly type was sitting off to the side in a wooden chair.

"Sí, mijita. Your hair is very pretty, too. I like the beads on your elastic bands." The short, stout woman had Chloe in her lap, and Chloe stroked a loose curl from the associate's bun.

"Chloe!" Tamara exclaimed.

"Hi, Tam," Chloe said, without taking her eyes off the woman.

"Is this your mami?" The associate's golden nametag read Yesinia, and the many stones on the mother's ring she wore indicated her multiple children and grand-children.

"That's my Tam. She's kind of like my mom now," Chloe replied. "How do you make your hair so red? Did it used to be brown?"

Tamara gave a nervous laugh. "Chloe, let's go home, sweetheart. You gave me a scare."

"No!" Chloe said, darting a glance at Tamara through narrowed eyes. "I want to stay here!" She wrapped her arms around the store associate's neck, burying her face in the woman's collar. "Can I go home with you?" she asked, her voice muffled. She pulled her head back, eyes bright. "Or do you want to come to my house? I can show you my room."

"I'm so sorry," Tamara said, at a loss.

The woman gave her a kind smile, but her eyes were concerned. "Is she always so friendly with strangers?" she asked softly. "When Diego, the security guard, brought her in, she was holding his hand like nothing."

"I know," Tamara said. "She's too trusting."

To Chloe, the store associate said, "It's very dangerous, preciosa. You need to be more careful." She tried to dis-entangle Chloe's arms from around her so that Tamara could pick her up, but the little girl was clinging tightly.

"I! Don't! Want! To! Go!" Chloe screamed.

Sweat prickled at Tamara's armpits. For all the world—again—it looked as though she were trying to steal this child from the arms of the woman she *really* loved. It took upwards of five minutes to separate Chloe from Yesinia, strands of the older woman's hair pulled from her bun in frizzy coils by Chloe's grasping fingers.

"I'm so sorry," Tamara said, rushing out with her wailing daughter. "I'm so sorry."

Chloe quieted almost instantly in the car, and Tamara pulled into the garage just as Chloe was rubbing her eyes.

"Naptime, Tam?" The little girl yawned in the backseat.

"Yes, baby. Let's get you in your bed." Tamara picked up the child and felt her warm weight on her chest. Chloe was limp and settled.

Inside, Tamara tucked Chloe into her pink butterfly bed, kissing her smooth forehead as the little girl's eyes fluttered with sleep.

She found Darryl in the living room, watching a football game.

"That was fast," he commented, without looking away from the television.

Tamara crossed in front of Darryl, blocking his view, and burst into tears.

"Whoa, whoa!" Darryl said. The first expression in his eyes was alarm, then a distant irritation. "What happened?"

Wiping her eyes and nose as she spoke, Tamara told her husband of her day with Chloe. How Chloe had run away at the first opportunity. How she'd found their daughter in the arms of a stranger, where she seemed perfectly content. How relieved she was that Chloe had opted to find a good person this time, and how terrified that she wouldn't find someone with such kind intentions the next.

"She was holding the security guard's hand—a *man*. I mean, Jesus, Darryl. She would've just walked out of the store with him, I know it. She wouldn't even think twice," Tamara said, starting to pull herself together. "And even though she's ours now, she isn't. Sometimes it seems like she can't be."

Darryl sighed. He stared at a spot on the carpet where Chloe had spilled grape juice; the stain lingered, though it sometimes looked like a shadow, something that might disappear in the light. "We don't know what we're doing here," Darryl said. "We've got to face that. I think it's time to call a psychologist, like Bianca recommended. Don't you?"

Tamara was out of arguments.

...

"Okay. What kind of insurance does the child have?" The receptionist's voice sounded underwhelmed.

Tamara immediately felt defensive. Because Chloe was technically adopted as a ward of the state, she would receive Medicaid benefits until her eighteenth birthday regardless of whether or not Tamara and Darryl added her to their private insurance. Tamara understood the stigma associated with Medicaid, especially for people of color. Although she tried to keep her voice casual, she could feel her adrenals in overdrive. She cleared her throat. "Medicaid," she said, trying to make it sound casual.

"I'm sorry. Dr. Finazzo does not accept Medicaid," the receptionist said.

"I see." Tamara hung up the phone before the call could go any further. She knew the condescending looks that people gave those on government assistance—the assumption that they were lazy or worthless. She felt heavy with a sense of sadness and indignation when she considered all the nasty thoughts that people who didn't know her circumstances or her life could have. Since Tamara had started her search based on a recommendation from another parent whose son had autism, she decided to instead scour the Internet and inform herself about Medicaid benefits for psychological care.

When she typed "Medicaid psychological benefits Wisconsin," she was overwhelmed by how many hits she got. She closed her eyes for a moment; even the *search* for help for her daughter seemed like an uphill battle. She composed herself, took a deep breath, and dove into the most promising sites.

On one, she found a table that she scrolled through until she found information about the Early Periodic Screening, Diagnosis, and Treatment (EPSDT) Mental Health Services. Clicking through, she saw that Medicaid would cover Chloe's expenses not only for evaluation, but also for psychotherapy, mental health day treatment, and specialized psychology. Relieved that her daughter would be eligible for not only the evaluation, but also any treatment that was prescribed by the psychologist, she read on. For services through Medicaid, the psychologist needed to submit a document for approval before evaluation and treatment services could begin. Only a diagnosis code from the EPSDT evaluation could be used for services. Even then, the psychologist needed to put in writing any information about the client's history, current presentation, and why services were required to address the diagnosis. Tamara thought that sounded overly complicated and had a feeling that the "prior approval" component, in particular, could prove tricky.

Not wanting to waste any more time, she decided to actually search for psychologists who accepted Medicaid. Dr. Margolis was the first psychologist who popped up, and was seemingly the only one within an hour's drive. After reading half a dozen five-star reviews online, Tamara called to make an appointment.

"Child Psychology Associates. This is Daisy. How can I help you?"

"Hi. My name is Tamara Ramsey, and I'm calling to schedule an appointment for my daughter, Chloe. I was hoping we could see Dr. Margolis." Tamara tried to sound confident, reassuring herself that Daisy heard this all day, every day; she was in no position to judge Tamara's family.

"Great. Chloe will need to get set up as a new patient in order for Dr. Margolis to perform the evaluation—and she does have availability, so you're in luck! If I could just get some background information from you, we can get started." Daisy's voice was professional but airy. Tamara thought she sounded more like a cheerleader than an office assistant, which might ordinarily annoy her but today was exactly what she needed.

"What's your daughter's full name?" Daisy asked.

"Chloe Imani Ramsey," Tamara replied. Saying Chloe's legal name aloud always made her feel better. Even though her daughter's name hadn't needed to be changed, the Ramsey part belonged to her and Darryl now.

"How old is Chloe?" Daisy asked, pecking away at a keyboard.

"She'll be five soon," Tamara answered.

"Oh! Kindergarten," Daisy said.

"Well, not quite. The school wants to hold her back a year," Tamara replied, almost apologetically.

"Oh. I'm sorry," Daisy said, and Tamara could feel the receptionist's embarrassment.

"No need to apologize. She would be entering kindergarten this year, but we agree with the school and have decided to hold her back. That's actually why I'm calling. Her teacher has some concerns, and my husband and I do, too." Tamara paused, not yet having polished her summary of Chloe's behavior and needs. "Chloe is our niece, whom we recently adopted. She had a rough go of things before she came to us. We need to check in with a professional to see if there's something we can do to better understand her and get things on track."

"Of course," Daisy said. "What kind of insurance does your daughter have?"

"Chloe has Medicaid." Tamara just spit it out so she didn't spend too much time in her head with it. "I know she needs preauthorization, but I'd like to get her in as soon as we can."

"Just one second . . ." Daisy seemed to be clicking around on her computer system. "Okay. The first session should be covered, and then we'll have to go from there with prior authorization for services, either a request for an evaluation or therapy. The next new patient appointment that Dr. Margolis has available is July twenty-third at ten a.m."

"July!" Tamara gasped. "But it's not even Memorial Day yet!"

"I know," Daisy said regretfully. "Unfortunately, she is booked solid. I can give you this appointment and put you on our list to contact in the event of a cancellation if you'd like."

"Okay. That's fine." Tamara sighed.

"Excellent. If I could get your contact info, I'll mail you

our intake paperwork to complete prior to the appointment. It includes an intake form, informed consent for patients' rights form, and a HIPAA form. You can expect it by the end of the week."

"Sure," Tamara said. As she spouted off her basic information, she said a silent prayer that someone would cancel their appointment in the next few weeks.

. . .

"We're waiting to get in to the psychologist. The appointment is next week, finally," Tamara said to Bianca. In addition to a parent rating scale, one of the forms that Dr. Margolis's office had requested was a behavior rating scale from a teacher regarding Chloe's behavior in the classroom. Tamara didn't just want to hear about what Bianca had to say on a form; she wanted to sit and talk with the woman who cared for her daughter while she was working, so she'd scheduled an appointment.

"I understand. It's not always easy to get in quickly to see a psychologist," Bianca said sympathetically. "And none of this has been easy or what you expected. You and Darryl are great parents. I see the love in your eyes."

"Thank you. It's especially not easy to get in to a psychologist when your daughter has insurance that many of them don't accept, especially for psychological testing and evaluation." Tamara took a deep breath. She felt Bianca's hand on her shoulder, providing a little comfort, and it was almost more than she could stand. Surprising even herself, Tamara suddenly released the emotion that she'd been storing.

Darryl had been more than distant lately. She could see the fear in his eyes when Chloe ran around the house in a frenzy, as though she were on a rabid sugar high, or when she yelled and threw toys when she wasn't happy with something. She could see the reluctance in his smile in family photos, even though that smile was plastered across his face. She wasn't sure where he was most of the time. He had started spending late nights at the office, or at least he said he was, but Tamara never knew which projects he was working on, and his checks weren't reflecting any overtime. As desperately as Tamara had wanted to become a parent, she now felt practically like a single mother to a child she didn't understand.

"I can't imagine how difficult this is." Bianca's voice was soft. "You're doing a great job, Tamara."

Tamara couldn't even respond. She'd unleashed something that had been buried just a little too long.

"Here is the form for the psychologist's office. You have my very best wishes. She's a wonderful child, and I'm excited to see how she benefits and continues growing through this next adventure," Bianca said. Clearly, she wasn't sure how to respond to Tamara's emotion, and Tamara felt awkward about putting her in a position where the line was blurred between personal and professional.

Tamara sniffed and nodded. "Thank you. I'm anxious and excited to see what this psychologist says."

Bianca smiled. "Me, too." She handed her paper to Tamara and stood to end the meeting. Tamara held herself together long enough to get into her car, where she promptly lost it. She called in sick to work, drove home, and crawled back into bed.

The last time she'd spent the afternoon in bed was when her college boyfriend had broken up with her. God, that had been fifteen years ago. Tamara rolled over onto

Darryl's pillow. She breathed in the scent of his after-shave and deodorant, and her senses were flooded with all the nights she'd spent enveloped in his fragrance. She remembered the way he'd looked in her eyes and told her what a wonderful mother she'd be. How he'd dreamed of a family with her. But none of their fantasies looked anything like this. Now the dreams they'd spent so many sleepy nights unfurling seemed almost silly, like two kids playing bride and groom, their feet engulfed by their parents' shoes.

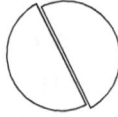

CHAPTER 4

Tamara reached for Darryl's hand as they walked into Dr. Michelle Margolis's office. She was expecting a bleak and clinical waiting room but was pleasantly surprised to find a collection of soft, child-sized Pottery Barn chairs arranged in a semicircle around a small television that was playing Disney Junior. Stacked on the side wall was a collection of children's and young adult storybooks. A play kitchen and matchbox racetrack were set up opposite the receptionist's desk. Chloe looked around the room indifferently. She was never excited by toys. Tamara didn't know why that still caught her off guard. The relief she felt at finally being here was quickly replaced by dread when she again realized how different Chloe was from other children.

Daisy, a petite woman in her midforties with almost crimson hair, smiled at Tamara and Darryl as they surveyed the room. "May I help you?" she asked.

"Chloe, don't you want to watch TV?" Tamara asked gently, ushering her daughter to the small chairs and walking toward Daisy's smile.

"I'm Tamara Ramsey. This is my husband, Darryl," Tamara said.

Daisy nodded at Darryl, and Tamara handed her the

paperwork she'd painstakingly completed.

Daisy looked over the packet and smiled. "This looks great. Thank you so much. If you'd like to have a seat, I'll bring this back to Dr. Margolis and she'll be right with you."

Tamara nodded, and she and Darryl walked over to the adult-sized black chairs across from the corner bin of oversized Legos, where Chloe had moved. Immediately, Darryl became engrossed in his phone. Tamara put her hand on his knee, hoping to get some affection, or at least acknowledgment that they were in this together. He glanced up from his phone and gave her a closed-lip smile before returning to his task.

"Could I ask you to be present today?" Tamara asked softly. "This could be emotional for us all and especially difficult for Chloe." She tried to keep her voice neutral, to guard Daisy (who'd again taken her seat) and Chloe (who was wandering over to the bookcase) from her thoughts.

"Well, because I had to take the day off work in the middle of our busiest time, I still need to have part of my brain at the office," Darryl replied curtly, his thumbs moving quickly.

Tamara decided to let it go. She didn't have the energy to defend her perspective against Darryl's. She was so worn out from working and taking care of Chloe that her marital problems were relegated to a constant sick feeling in her stomach.

"Tamara and Darryl?" A voice broke Tamara's thoughts, and she looked up to see a woman, Dr. Margolis, smiling at the door to the waiting room. With dark, curly hair clipped into a low ponytail, Dr. Margolis had the remarkable genes of South American descent, those genes that kept her age a secret, save for tiny laugh lines around her eyes.

"That's us." Tamara stood. "Chloe, baby. Come on."

"If you don't mind, I'd like for Chloe to sit out here for a few minutes while the three of us have a chat. Daisy can keep an eye on her." Dr. Margolis smiled, her slight accent lending a poetic lilt to her voice.

Tamara nodded. "Chloe," she called, "we'll be back in just a minute. Be good for Ms. Daisy."

Chloe hardly even glanced up from the Legos as Tamara and Darryl followed Dr. Margolis out of the room.

In Dr. Margolis's office, the couple took seats on either side of a pine desk while the psychologist took a seat in the middle, triangulating them. Tamara was suddenly hot. She wanted to slip her feet from her sandals and place them on the cool white tile.

"I've reviewed all of Chloe's paperwork," Dr. Margolis said. "Great job putting it together, you two."

Tamara smiled and stifled the reflex to tell the psychologist that *she'd* put it all together. "Thank you."

"So, today will just be a brief discussion to review more of your daughter's history, what you're seeing at home, and what the teachers are reporting at school. Then I'd like to spend some time alone with Chloe. From there, we will wrap things up for now and discuss next steps. Sound good?"

Tamara nodded and looked over to Darryl, who also gave a brief nod.

"From reviewing the records that you sent," Dr. Margolis said, "I see that Chloe is adopted, and it clearly wasn't under the best circumstances."

Tamara paused and waited for Darryl to take over,

but after a pregnant silence, she launched into what she knew of Chloe's early life: Jasmine's neglect, Chloe's environment, and finally the circumstances under which Chloe had come to live with them. She described the time between then and now at home and at school, and when she'd finished the story, Dr. Margolis looked into Tamara's eyes.

"It's good that Chloe has you both in her life," she said. "You're good parents to bring her here."

Tamara swallowed hard. "Thank you."

"Okay, it looks like you've fully completed all the paperwork and rating scales. Right now I'd like to spend some time with your daughter, so if you don't mind, I'm going to ask you both to return to the waiting room."

Tamara cast Darryl a mystified glance. "She's so young," she said to Dr. Margolis. "I don't know how much of her experience she'll be able to communicate . . ."

Dr. Margolis smiled. "You're exactly right. Children don't yet verbally communicate the way that we do, but interacting with children as they play—and observing how they play—is a window into their world."

Nondirective play therapy is a counseling method used to help children communicate their inner experiences through the use of toys and play.

In the waiting room, Chloe had left Legos and stuffed animals and books strewn haphazardly across the floor. Tamara said, "Chloe! What have we discussed about putting our toys away when we're done using them? I'm sorry," she said to Dr. Margolis.

Dr. Margolis smiled. "Don't worry. Chloe?" she called. "Hi! I'm Michelle. Would you like to come color with me?"

Chloe's deep brown eyes illuminated with her smile. "Yeah!" she said, running to hug the psychologist tightly across her knees.

Dr. Margolis left the doors open between the waiting room and her office, allowing Tamara and Darryl to watch the scene unfold down the hall. When Dr. Margolis sat, Chloe climbed into her lap and stroked her cheek. Kindly, but firmly, Dr. Margolis sat her little client on the chair next to her. From her desk, she took a sheet of white paper and a box of crayons and handed them to Chloe.

Tamara looked at Darryl, hoping that he was as engaged as she was in watching this interaction, but when she saw him again replying to emails on his phone, she lost her temper.

"Oh, for God's sake, Darryl. Put your phone down!" Tamara said, glaring at him. "Is it too much to ask that you're actually here, paying attention to us?"

"I'm here, Tamara. I'm always here," Darryl responded, his tone sharp. "What do you need, darling, because I'm right here. For you."

A cold rage washed over Tamara, and before she went blackout angry, she opted to take a breath. "You selfish son of a bitch. You have *no* idea what life has been like for me the past year, do you? You've been so busy with all the things that keep you out of the house. When you are home, you're so disengaged that I often wish you weren't around providing a distraction." Her voice was a hissing whisper that Daisy must have been pretending not to hear.

Darryl's eyes narrowed. "You're right. I have no idea what life is like for you. Ever since Chloe came into our home, you've shut me out of everything. I don't matter to you at all anymore. All you care about is bonding with Chloe, fixing things for her, going to work. You're obsessed. You're not interested in being a co-parent; you're interested in having complete control over everything. You're interested in shutting me out. I've disengaged because there is nothing here for me to engage with."

His words cut Tamara to the core. She was angry, but she couldn't help but see that he had a point, if an exaggerated one. She sank back into herself, spending the next five minutes in silence until a shriek drove her from her seat.

"No!" Chloe was screaming. "I'm not done! I don't want to stop!"

Tamara was halfway down the hall when she saw Dr. Margolis gesture for her to stay back. Caught between wanting to soothe her daughter and not wanting to interfere, Tamara stayed frozen until Darryl came and softly took her elbow. Silently, they walked back to their seats.

They sat tensely for fifteen more minutes, during which Chloe went from screaming to giggling. Finally, Dr. Margolis appeared in the doorway and motioned them back into her office. Chloe wandered over to Daisy, asking if she wanted to play.

Dr. Margolis broke the silence as the three of them walked together toward her office. "Chloe is a bright little girl with a lot of potential, and in some ways that makes this even harder. Thank you for coming today. That took courage."

Tamara nodded, pushing her fight with Darryl to the back of her mind. For a moment, she wondered how he was doing with this, but she couldn't bring herself to look at him now.

CHAPTER 4

"I know this is only our first visit and I still have quite a bit to learn about your daughter. But right now, based on what you are telling me, meeting with her, and reviewing her history, I'm starting to wonder about a trauma or stressor-related disorder. I know that's challenging to hear," Dr. Margolis said kindly. "But I'd like to submit the paperwork for psychological testing. It may take some time. I'd like to set another appointment for three weeks from now."

"What kind of trauma or stressor-related disorder?" Tamara asked. "Like PTSD?" It was the only thing that came to mind, and she'd always associated it with veterans, like her father, whose minds never quite left the war where they'd changed.

"Not exactly," Dr. Margolis said. "I'd like to spend more time with Chloe before considering a formal diagnosis, but I suspect that the change of caregivers—from her mother to her grandmother, back to her mother—coupled with the neglect she experienced in her early life impacted the way she attaches to others. Again, I'd like to spend more time with her to be sure."

"Yes. Of course. Thank you." Tamara rose and extended her hand for a handshake. Darryl followed, and the couple collected their little girl and silently drove her to school for the afternoon before returning home.

Tamara emerged from her closet in a pair of baggy sweatpants and a t-shirt from her latest company picnic. While she hadn't anticipated having the afternoon to herself, it seemed that while she'd been changing clothes, Darryl had gone back to work. She went into the kitchen and started to unload the dishwasher when she saw him sitting on their back porch with a can of

Diet Coke. Sliding on her sandals, she opened the door and joined him.

"I'm sorry," she said, lowering her eyes. "I've been in this daze ever since we brought Chloe home. It was all so unexpected, and I've just been trying to do my best for her. I don't like what it's done to us, though."

Darryl set down the newspaper that he'd been reading. "That's the most you've said to me in months."

"It's not for lack of trying." Tamara's voice was sharper than she'd intended, but she didn't know what else to say. Yes, she shared the blame in the creation of the vast space between her and Darryl, but she'd just apologized.

"I'm sorry, too. I wasn't ready for this. Typically, men get nine months to figure out where they land on the totem pole when their family grows to three. I got about nine minutes. And I lost my sister. Chloe looks just like her when we were little. She . . ." Darryl's voice cracked. "She has that damaged look in her eyes. Jasmine was a beautiful person, but something was just off about her after Daddy died. I couldn't save Jasmine. I tried. In high school, I pounded the bastards who bragged about sleeping with her. I drove around in the middle of the night to find her. I made her detox at my apartment in college so Mama didn't see her. I cleaned up her vomit. And now we have her kid, and I'm terrified . . ." Overwhelmed with emotion, Darryl trailed off.

Suddenly, Tamara felt terrible for never making the connection between Darryl and his sister, and Darryl and Chloe. His reaction to Jasmine's death had seemed so cavalier, but with Chloe's arrival, he'd never had time to mourn. With that realization, Tamara leaned into her husband, wrapping her arms around his neck while his warm tears wet the front of her t-shirt. They sat outside that way, without another word, until they both went to pick Chloe up from school.

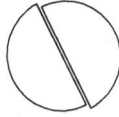

CHAPTER 5

Tamara was loading the dishwasher while Chloe and Darryl watched an episode of *Mickey Mouse Clubhouse* that had been sitting on the DVR for a few days. From the living room, Tamara heard Chloe tell Darryl, "You're not going to the secret clubhouse, because you didn't say 'Miksa Mooska Mickey Mouse!' You have to say it, Daddy!" Tamara's heart leaped at the word *Daddy*.

After she and Darryl had reconnected on their back porch that day, he'd been making a more concerted effort with Chloe, and the couple had started to refer to themselves as Mama and Daddy. While nine times out of ten, Chloe still called her "Mam" instead of the "Tam" she was used to, Tamara was thrilled that it was taking.

Their second visit with Dr. Margolis was similar to the first, although, at the end, Chloe had run off to play with the Legos. Finally, after their third visit, Dr. Margolis had a frank conversation with the couple about the diagnosis she'd reached.

"Disinhibited social engagement disorder, or DSED, is a new condition outlined by the DSM-5," Dr. Margolis said. "It used to be classified as the disinhibited form of reactive attachment disorder, or RAD, but its unique diagnostic criteria make it a diagnosis unto itself."

"What is that?" Tamara asked. "After we adopted Chloe, I read about reactive attachment disorder, but that actually seemed opposite to what we were experiencing with her. At first, I thought we were lucky . . ." Tamara trailed off.

Dr. Margolis nodded. "DSED and reactive attachment disorder are born from similar conditions: extreme abuse or neglect in a child's early years, before two years of age. Both are attachment disorders; the child does not know how to form proper bonds or social connections with others. But while children with RAD are often stuck in frozen watchfulness, extremely mistrusting of the world around them, kids with DSED attach indiscriminately. She's familiar with you, but she'll cling to almost anyone in a way that's culturally and socially inappropriate. She won't hesitate to climb onto strangers' laps, to play with their hair, even to hug and kiss them. Naturally, this makes her vulnerable to those with bad intentions, but as she grows older, it will also directly impact the relationships she forms."

Diagnostic criteria for *disinhibited social engagement disorder*:

A. A pattern of behavior in which a child actively approaches and interacts with unfamiliar adults and exhibits at least two of the following:

1. Reduced or absent reticence in approaching and interacting with unfamiliar adults

2. Overly familiar verbal and physical behavior (that is not consistent with culturally sanctioned and age-appropriate social boundaries)

3. Diminished or absent checking back with adult caregiver after venturing away, even in unfamiliar settings

4. Willingness to go off with unfamiliar adults with minimal or no hesitation

B. The behaviors in criterion A are not limited to impulsivity (as in attention deficit hyperactivity disorder), but include socially disinhibited behavior.

C. The child has experienced a pattern of extremes of insufficient care as evidenced by at least one of the following:

1. Social neglect or deprivation in the form of persistent lack of having basic emotional needs for comfort, stimulation, and affection met by caregiving adults

2. Repeated changes of primary caregivers that limit opportunities to form stable attachments (e.g., frequent changes in foster care)

3. Rearing in unusual settings that severely limit opportunities to form selective attachments (e.g., institutions with high child-to-caregiver ratios)

D. The care in criterion C is presumed to be responsible for the disturbed behavior in criterion A (e.g., the disturbances in criterion A began after the pathogenic care in criterion C).

E. The child has a developmental age of at least nine months.

Specify if:

Persistent: The disorder has been present for more than twelve months.

Specify current severity:

Disinhibited social engagement disorder is specified as **severe** when the child manifests all symptoms of the disorder, with each symptom manifesting at relatively high levels.

41

Tamara's head was reeling. She could so easily imagine Chloe climbing into the back of a van, never to be seen again.

"What about her other behavior?" Darryl asked. "Bianca, her teacher, has been direct with us about the disruption Chloe causes in the classroom. She seems to be all over the place, unable to focus on one task for long, but she also doesn't like being forced to switch activities before she's ready. And that's an understatement."

Dr. Margolis nodded. "Because of its association with early social neglect, DSED often co-occurs with developmental delays, especially cognitive and language development. In this case, I believe Chloe is struggling with attention deficit hyperactivity disorder," she said. "ADHD explains the shifts in her attention span and her inability to understand how to follow instructions."

> *Attention deficit hyperactivity disorder* (ADHD) is one of the most common childhood disorders and can continue through adolescence and adulthood. Symptoms include difficulty staying focused and paying attention, difficulty controlling behavior, and hyperactivity (overactivity).

For a few moments, the room was silent. Tamara found herself thinking of her own childhood: Once, she'd gotten lost at an amusement park. She was five or six, desperately searching strangers' faces, certain her parents would never find her, terrified. She'd had nightmares for months, and her parents took turns letting her fall back asleep in the crook of their arms. Tamara had known implicitly who was safe; it boggled her mind to think that Chloe, in that same situation, would feel no fear—that they, her parents, were no different to her than Daisy in the waiting room.

"I'm almost relieved," Darryl said, his voice brusque with emotion. "I don't know why naming what's wrong with Chloe seems to help, but it does."

Dr. Margolis nodded. "A lot of parents feel that way. When something is named, it becomes observable in a new way. It becomes externally understood."

"Is it treatable?" Tamara blurted. "I'm sorry, I'm glad you're relieved, Darryl, but this is just overwhelming."

Darryl placed a warm hand on Tamara's knee. "What are our next steps?" he asked Dr. Margolis.

"I recommend individual therapy with Chloe and behavioral consultation with you two. We can begin our sessions immediately." Dr. Margolis paused. "Depending on the progress we see, I may also recommend a consultation with a child and adolescent psychiatrist."

> A *child and adolescent psychiatrist* is an individual with a medical degree (M.D.), licensed by individual states to practice psychiatry. He or she can provide evaluations, as well as treat emotional and behavioral problems and mental disorders by prescribing psychotropic medications and by providing other psychotherapeutic techniques.

"A psychiatrist?" Tamara asked, looking between Dr. Margolis and Darryl. "Psychiatrists prescribe medications, don't they? Are you saying you think we need to medicate Chloe?"

"Medication is always a last resort," Dr. Margolis said, "so again, it may not be necessary. But depending on how Chloe responds to the therapy, you may appreciate some immediate symptom relief for the ADHD—if Chloe is less distractible, less impulsive, she's able to be more available for therapy. And remember," she added, "just because you see a psychiatrist for an evaluation doesn't mean that medication is a foregone conclusion."

> **Psychotropic medications** are any medications used to treat mental disorders. There are many types of psychotropic medications, including antidepressants, anxiolytics, mood stabilizers, stimulants, and antipsychotics.

Later, Tamara thought about this conversation. She was not against medication in the general sense; she never hesitated to raid her leftover antibiotics to self-treat a throat infection, and she had plenty of friends who had benefited from antidepressants. There had been times in her life when she thought she could use them as well. But Chloe was five. Her brain was still developing. How much of her behavior could be improved with therapy, with patience and love? And yet, if Chloe were, say, diabetic, no amount of love alone could cure her, and Tamara knew they wouldn't deny her insulin. Where was the line? Just as she lifted a pan with remnants of spaghetti sauce, the doorbell rang.

Stacy, Chloe's social worker, stood outside, briefcase in hand.

"What a surprise! Come on in, Stacy." Tamara smiled, despite her instant anxiety. Stacy had come to see the Ramseys periodically, just to ensure that the family was adjusting. As far as Tamara could tell, everything had appeared normal to Stacy so far—but nothing about this journey had been expected, so Tamara couldn't help feeling wary. She was also dreading the possibility of Chloe overly attaching to Stacy again.

"Thanks, Tamara. I'm just doing a drop-in visit. Checking in with you three." Stacy returned Tamara's smile and handshake.

"Darryl, Stacy is here," Tamara called into the living room. "Would you mind watching Chloe while I talk with her first?"

"Not at all. We're at the good part," Darryl laughed. "Come get me when you need us."

Stacy set up her laptop on the dining room table as Tamara poured glasses of water for them both.

"So how have things been going for you all?" Stacy asked, sitting down.

"Well, we took her to a psychologist for evaluation, as you know," Tamara said, joining Stacy at the table. "Her formal diagnosis was disinhibited social engagement disorder and ADHD."

"Yes, I got the evaluation from Dr. Margolis. Thank you for having her office send that over. And how have things been since then? What's the plan of action?" Stacy peered at Tamara over her laptop screen.

Tamara paused. There had been a subtle change in their home over the past two weeks, but she knew it had less to do with Chloe's evaluation and more to do with the conversation between her and Darryl. Without going into the specifics of how she and her husband were learning to work together as parents and partners, Tamara started.

"Well, we've come out of denial that Chloe's problems are something she will just grow out of," she said. "We're still dealing with all the same things, though. We have to keep such a sharp eye on her when we all leave the house, because I kid you not, Stacy, she would climb into the first car whose driver opened a door for her. It's terrifying. Her inattention and impulsivity are still a problem at school and home, but we want to try therapy for both before we consider medication. Next week is our first therapy session with Dr. Margolis. I don't know what to expect, but I at least feel that we're on the right track."

Stacy nodded, taking notes. "How often is therapy?"

"Once every two weeks, I think." Tamara frowned. Medicaid billing was so specific, and so many professionals had to watch every line and code they put in her charts to ensure that all the paperwork was uniform. "I wish there were more we could do. One hour every two weeks just doesn't seem like enough."

Stacy nodded, and then her eyes lit up. "You know what? We work with a number of community-based providers. One is called Oconomowoc Residential Programs. Although they have focused on residential care and day school for the past thirty years, they also have a community-based services program, which I think might be a great fit for your family. First, the team would do a family assessment to see about the alignment between your needs and what they can provide. Then, if approved, we could get services in your home."

Tamara was intrigued. "What do those services include?"

"Well, the team would work with Chloe and your family for a certain number of hours a week, usually about five, but that all depends on needs and funding. They usually provide a combination of individual sessions with the child and parents, education on disability characteristics, and behavioral consultations, as well as family-based services. They can also coordinate with the school and other providers to help with continuity of care." Stacy made another note in her laptop.

Tamara felt a crack of light opening in her chest. How much more help was out there for families like hers? How many parents struggled alone because they didn't know any better?

"How does the funding work?" Tamara asked.

"Well, you'd need to be approved for waiver funding, and you're still on the waiting list," Stacy said. "Waiver funding is Medicaid money that is allotted to the state specifically to fund services for kids who are still at home—it's not for residential placement, in other words. These programs are a realistic attempt to make it comfortable for kids to continue living at home despite being challenged in terms of emotional-behavioral-type problems.

"But since Chloe would be considered at risk for out-of-home placement . . ." Stacy continued, rapping a finger on the table as she seemed to think out loud, "it might be possible to utilize an emergency waiver slot and get you involved with an agency that contracts with Genesee Lake School. This way, you can definitely work with the community-based services team."

As she and Stacy finished their conversation, Tamara recognized the feeling that was making her heart beat a little quicker: hope.

"Stacy, that would be amazing," Tamara said, cringing as, out of nowhere, Chloe careened into the room. She stopped when she saw Stacy.

"*Stacy!*" Chloe yelled, running to the social worker. She climbed on Stacy's lap and wrapped her arms around her neck, burying her face against Stacy's clavicle. "Why haven't you come to visit me?" she asked, muffled against Stacy's shirt.

"Chloe," Tamara said, pushing her chair back. "Come here. Stacy was just about to get going."

"*No!*" Chloe shrieked when she felt Tamara's hands lift her. She tried squeezing her legs around Stacy's waist, but Stacy slid her chair back and firmly unpeeled the little girl's calves from their clutch.

Darryl stepped into the room, his face sheepish as he went to help Tamara. "I'm sorry," he said. "I got a work call. I stepped out for just a second—"

"It's okay," Tamara said, trying to keep her voice even as Chloe kicked and cried. "Just help me here."

Stacy was a quiet witness as Tamara and Darryl wrangled their child away from her. Her face was apologetic and compassionate as she began packing her laptop away.

"I'll check on that emergency waiver," she said softly to Tamara, as Darryl carried a wailing Chloe away.

• • •

Baskets stacked with toys were scattered throughout a large room, along with colorful removable mats. In the far left corner was a kitchen and home area, with baby dolls, plastic food, and a small dining table. In the opposite corner, a table was set up with art supplies, Play-Doh, paints, paper, and markers. The walls were painted a bright yellow, which was muted by the dark finish of the hardwood floor beneath the mats. Part of their first therapy visit with Dr. Margolis was play.

Chloe dashed toward the Play-Doh table without even a look back at her parents. Tamara bit her lip but smiled at Dr. Margolis.

Dr. Margolis gave them an understanding smile. "Chloe's making herself right at home. Now, as we've discussed before, enhancement of caregiving quality is one part of addressing the course of DSED. Chloe needs to relearn the relationship between herself and her primary caregivers."

"Right," Tamara said. "Making up for Jasmine. Sorry," she said to Darryl.

Darryl nodded. "What can we do?" he asked Dr. Margolis.

"Right now, I'd like to join Chloe for some nondirective play with a dollhouse. Our goal, over time, will be to cultivate a normalization of what it means to be Mommy, Daddy, family. But for right now, I just want to see where she goes. If you don't mind, I'll ask you two to wait outside. You can watch through the window." Dr. Margolis smiled at them before walking over to the kitchen center, where Chloe had started to examine, more than play, with the structure.

"Chloe," Dr. Margolis said, "your mom and dad are going to leave now. Do you want to say goodbye?"

Chloe glanced up, indifferent. Though the response was expected, it still stung. By the wounded flash in Darryl's eyes, Tamara knew she wasn't alone. Quietly, she took his hand and they left the room, observing from seats before a large window.

Kneeling down, Dr. Margolis pointed to the doll that Chloe was holding by the foot as she threw plastic food into a basket.

"Tell me about the baby," she said, smiling.

"Why?" Chloe asked, continuing to scour the pantry.

"The baby looks a little uncomfortable," Dr. Margolis said, tilting her head. "How should people hold babies?"

Chloe looked over her shoulder at Dr. Margolis and shrugged, tossing the doll into the plastic crib that was set up between the kitchen and the plastic dining table.

"Should we rock the baby or give her a bottle?" Dr. Margolis asked.

Chloe shook her head. "No."

"Why not?" Dr. Margolis asked.

Chloe didn't answer.

"Chloe?" Dr. Margolis prodded gently.

Chloe grabbed the baby from the crib, her tiny fingers wrapped around its ankle. She stared at the baby with an indecipherable look on her face. Then she raised it above her head and smacked it onto the ground. She looked up at Dr. Margolis and laughed. "Pow!" she said. She laughed and did it again, then a third time.

"Chloe, don't you think we should be more gentle with—"

Chloe hurled the doll across the room and yelled, "I don't want to play with the baby! The baby's stupid! I want to play with . . ." Her eyes scanned the room. "Play-Doh!" She scurried on all fours toward the table on the opposite wall, opening one small container of Play-Doh after the next and upturning them onto the table.

Dr. Margolis joined Chloe. "Can I play, too?" she asked.

Chloe glanced up, then back at the colorful mounds in front of her, which she was pounding into patties. "Okay," she said.

When Dr. Margolis attempted to reach for an unopened jar of Play-Doh, Chloe shrieked.

"No!" she yelled, swatting at Dr. Margolis's hand. "That one's mine! You have to use your own!"

"Okay, Chloe," Dr. Margolis said. Her voice was low and soothing, as though she was entirely unperturbed by Chloe's behavior. "Why don't we—"

Without a word, Chloe rose from the tiny chair she had occupied and ran across the room, grabbing a bright hardcover book from a basket. "Can you read me a story?" she asked. The words were sweet, but Chloe was nearly yelling, frenetic. She opened the book and pushed from one page to the next so quickly that Tamara winced, fearing she'd rip them.

After a few more minutes, Dr. Margolis motioned for Tamara and Darryl to join them, and Tamara took a few calming breaths before standing. Darryl was glued to his seat, unable to move.

When Tamara knelt beside Chloe, Dr. Margolis handed her the discarded doll. "Mom, would you show Chloe how you hold the baby?"

Tamara collected the doll carefully, taking care to support her head. She held the cold plastic form close to her chest, rocking back and forth and humming a song.

Chloe snatched the doll away from her mother. With a mischievous look on her face, she reared her arm back and again thwacked the doll onto the floor. She giggled.

"Chloe, don't you think you're being a little rough with the baby?" Tamara asked.

Chloe's face grew sullen. "It's funny."

"I'm sorry," Tamara said to Dr. Margolis. "I don't know what I'm supposed to be doing here."

Quietly, Dr. Margolis said, "Why don't we let Daisy watch Chloe for a few minutes while we have a conversation?"

In Dr. Margolis's office, the psychologist said, "That was probably troubling to watch. How are you both feeling?"

Darryl sighed and rubbed his hands over his head. "Like I want to raise my sister from the dead so I can shake her," he said, his voice muffled as he lowered his face into his palms.

"For the first time, I got a clear picture of what Bianca has experienced with Chloe in the classroom," Tamara said. She felt a rush of gratitude for the teacher, who had always been so willing to work with Chloe, despite the obvious difficulties.

"Yes, the lack of engagement, distractibility, and hyperactivity are a bit of a challenge here," Dr. Margolis said carefully. "I don't want to push you two in a direction you're not comfortable with, but again, I think you might consider a referral to a child and adolescent psychiatrist. Medication—the right medication, in the right dosage—can help Chloe be more available for therapy."

Darryl lifted his face from his hands and looked at Tamara. She nodded.

"We'll take the referral," Darryl said.

Dr. Margolis nodded, and Darryl and Tamara thanked her and made another appointment in two weeks' time.

After dropping Chloe off at school, Darryl broke the car-ride silence. "We haven't talked about it, but how do you feel about medication?"

"Like I never thought I'd have to form an opinion on it," Tamara said, staring out the window. When Darryl didn't respond, she sighed. "A part of me hates the idea. Chloe's brain has been through enough, hasn't it, without adding who knows what chemicals to it? But at the same time, if there's something out there that can really help her, how can I possibly say no?"

Darryl nodded, his jaw tense. "Yeah. I'm in the same place. You know, after Jasmine got out of rehab once when we were younger, she was diagnosed with depression and started taking meds. I think she stayed sober three or four months, and I don't know if it was that or the antidepressants, but she seemed . . . lighter. Better. I really thought there was a chance, you know, that if depression was the real cause of her risky behavior, meds could help her stay clean by addressing it better than drugs and booze."

"What happened?" Tamara asked.

"Well, she may have been better, but she was still Jasmine. She confronted her supervisor for what she said was a lewd comment, lost her job, lost her insurance, stopped being able to pay for the meds. It was back to working at a bar. It wasn't long after that."

Tamara felt numb and heavy. The therapy session had gone so badly, and she'd had such high hopes. But maybe Darryl was right. Chloe had been dealt a hard hand biologically and environmentally; medication had seemed to help her mother, albeit briefly. Maybe it could help her, too.

"We have the meeting with the in-home services people this afternoon," Tamara said, feeling a rush of gratitude toward Stacy, who had been able to get them the emergency waiver. "Let's hope that goes better. We'll cross the medication road when we get there."

"You mean tomorrow?" Darryl said, half-joking, making Tamara laugh despite herself.

When they got home, Tamara worked to straighten up the house while Darryl tried to reach Dr. Harris, the psychiatrist Dr. Margolis had recommended. He left a message with the receptionist, stating that they needed to get Chloe in ASAP. The phone rang just when Tamara and Darryl were expecting Cynthia, the community services coordinator, and Dr. Pham, the program's psychologist, to arrive.

"Hi, Darryl. This is Bianca Carter." Chloe's teacher's voice was strained, and Darryl's heart sank.

"Hey, Bianca, what's going on?" he asked.

"Chloe's only been at school for an hour, but she hasn't stopped being disruptive. She's running around the classroom, knocking things away from the other students. She started as soon as you and Tamara left, and she's absolutely out of control. I've tried everything I can think of to calm her down, but it's not working. I don't know what to do with her." Bianca sounded breathless. "We have her in the administrator's office while the other kids are down for a nap, but she's bouncing off the walls. I'm sorry, but we need you to come get her." Almost as an afterthought, Bianca added, "Did something happen today?"

"We had our first therapy session this morning, and I wonder if that . . ." Darryl trailed off. How could he tell Bianca that the therapy that was supposed to help Chloe could have triggered this tantrum? How could he help her understand things that *he* didn't even comprehend? The powerlessness Darryl felt was enough to make him want to punch a wall.

Just then the doorbell rang. "Bianca, we have an appointment that just got here for Chloe. I have to go. I'll be there as soon as I can." Darryl hung up the phone before the overwhelmed teacher could respond.

Tamara opened the door to Cynthia and Dr. Pham with a big, forced smile. She was relieved that they were there, but after that morning, she found herself skeptical that anything would work for Chloe and their family.

Cynthia, a tall woman with long nutmeg-brown hair, smiled warmly and shook Tamara's hand. Behind her, Dr. Pham's dark hair shone almost purple in the sun behind her. She followed Cynthia, and when Darryl came in to greet the women, he immediately apologized.

"I just got a call from the school," he explained, looking meaningfully at Tamara. "Chloe isn't having a great day. Tamara will fill you in on what you need to know, and I'll be back as soon as I can."

Tamara nodded before leading the women to her dining table.

"Can I get anyone anything? Some coffee or tea?" she offered as they all took their seats.

"No, I think we're good." Dr. Pham smiled back at Tamara. "Thank you for having us over today. I've received all of Chloe's paperwork from her social worker, and we've had a chance to look over her reports as well as comments and observations from you and from her teachers. Today, we'd like to learn more about your daughter and discuss how we see our services working for your family. As you know, our focus is to work as a team with all of her other care providers. I saw that she is also working with a licensed clinical psychologist. Have you begun the therapy yet?"

Tamara gave a sad smile. "Yes. We started this morning. It was not good."

"What do you mean?" Dr. Pham asked.

Tamara gave the play-by-play of the thirty minutes they'd spent with Dr. Margolis. Dr. Pham nodded and took notes.

When Tamara finished speaking, Cynthia asked her, "If things were better here for your family, how would that 'look' for you?"

Tamara took a deep breath. "I just want Chloe to be able to feel our love. I know she's had it rough and that I can't erase the first four years of her life. But I would like for her to be in a place where the events that burden her are background noise behind her successful life. We've tried so hard, given her everything that we can, and she still doesn't understand that we love her." Tamara's voice cracked. "I get that what she learned early on about people, herself, and the world skewed her perceptions. But the fact that I could walk out the door and never come back and I don't even think she'd care . . . That's hard. It's really hard. And yet, of course, it makes sense."

Tamara continued, feeling as though she was babbling but unable to stop. "Then there's the ADHD behavior. It's exhausting. I know kids have a lot of energy, but she's something else. That's probably why her teacher called. Bianca's a saint," she said, "but even saints have their limits."

Cynthia nodded, and Dr. Pham spoke. "It sounds like it's been very challenging for you three."

Tamara nodded, swallowing hard. "We're pretty desperate," she admitted quietly. "Something needs to go right here. Please—I'd love to know how you think you can help."

Dr. Pham said, "What we'd like to see is a lot of good interaction between you, your husband, and Chloe. Sessions will help you understand the impact of complex developmental trauma on Chloe and work to build healthy and healing relationships. Over time, it will improve attachment, bonding, and relational health, as well as self-regulation and problem-solving skills."

"That all sounds amazing," Tamara said, looking from one woman to the other. "But—how?"

"One hour a week, we'll have someone work directly with you and your husband to provide education about the disabilities—it's pretty tough to try to fix something we don't fully understand." Dr. Pham smiled, and Tamara nodded. "We'll also provide behavior management strategies as far as the DSED and ADHD go. In the context of

ADHD, that might include, for example, teaching organizational skills. Having a routine and structure. Using a daily visual schedule."

A *daily visual schedule* is an important aspect of a structured environment. Visual schedules tell children what activities will occur and in what order. They can help address a child's difficulty with sequential memory and organization of time, as well as quiet anxieties about not knowing what to expect next. Visual schedules can also help children learn to transition independently between activities.

Cynthia nodded, adding, "We teach collaborative problem solving and help children regulate with various tools. I work with a boy who hasn't been formally diagnosed with a trauma disorder but has the history, and we've taught him an emotional scale—one through five—to help him communicate with us where he is. Once we know he's a four, really dysregulated, we can help him self-calm. Things like that. Chloe gets agitated and angry?" she asked.

Collaborative problem solving is an approach based on two major principles: first, that a child's challenges are "best understood as the byproduct of lagging thinking skills (rather than, for example, as attention-seeking, manipulative, limit-testing, or a sign of poor motivation); and second, that these challenges are best addressed by teaching children the skills they lack (rather than through reward and punishment programs and intensive imposition of adult will)."

Tamara nodded. "Does she ever," she said dryly.

"Okay, great—we can help her start to understand her own cycle: what her triggers are, how her body feels when she's getting upset. We can give her tools and strategies to self-regulate."

Tamara was in awe. "Yes!" she said. "This is exactly what we're looking for. But what about the attachment aspect? The ADHD is probably more disruptive, but the DSED is terrifying. That's what we really don't know how to deal with."

"We can help you engage in repetition and positive relationship-building experiences," Cynthia said, "as well as reinforce appropriate boundaries and teach Chloe social skills through community outings. The nice thing about that," she added, "is it gives you a bit of respite, even if it's only an hour or so at a time."

"An hour to myself?" Tamara exclaimed, only half joking. "I don't know what I'd do with it!"

Cynthia and Dr. Pham chuckled. "So," Dr. Pham said, "does this sound in alignment with your needs?"

"Yes!" Tamara practically shouted. "We're only scheduled for fifty minutes with Dr. Margolis every two weeks, and I just don't think it's nearly enough."

"Unfortunately, it's not for many families," Dr. Pham said.

"Well, I'll catch my husband up on everything we've talked about," Tamara said, suddenly worried about what Darryl might be facing at the school and whether he had called; her cell phone was still buried in her purse. "But I'm ready to begin, and I'm sure he will be, too. What are the next steps?"

"Cynthia will assign your family a lead clinical coordinator. Under my supervision, Chloe's lead will work with behavior support specialists, additional staff that help to implement the treatment plan we devise."

"Thank you," Tamara said, relieved, almost more than anything, to have her hope reignited.

· · ·

When Darryl walked into the office at Chloe's school, Bianca was waiting for him. Her eyes were glassy, her hair disheveled.

"Hey, Darryl," she said. "Chloe is with the school nurse now."

Darryl could hear Chloe's screams through the closed door to the right.

"I can hear her," he said quietly.

Bianca nodded. "You're in a rough spot, Darryl. I don't mean to make it worse, but I need to let you know—I had to talk to the principal about Chloe's behavior."

Darryl nodded, dreading the next part of Bianca's speech.

"If things don't improve over the next month, I'm worried that the principal will need to make some tough choices."

"You mean ask us to leave," Darryl said.

Bianca nodded, pressing her lips together. "I'm so sorry."

Darryl, numbed by another sucker punch of bad news, just nodded back. "We're taking her to see a psychiatrist as soon as he calls us back. Tamara is meeting with the in-home services team as we speak. Things have to turn around, Bianca." He was trying to convince himself as much as her. He didn't want Chloe's life to change drastically again. She was at her school nearly forty hours a week as he and Tamara both worked. She loved it there, she loved Bianca, and Darryl didn't want to pull her away from anything that was comfortable in the midst of so much other change.

Bianca nodded. "I hope so. And I'm your ally here.

I want you to know that."

"I know," Darryl said. "We appreciate that."

Darryl offered her a tight smile before following Chloe's wails to the door.

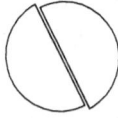

CHAPTER 6

Dr. Harris was the psychiatrist Dr. Margolis had recommended. Despite his best efforts, Darryl couldn't reschedule a work meeting, so Tamara sat with Chloe on the stiff leather chairs in the waiting room, trying to keep her daughter on task with the coloring book and crayons that she had stashed in her oversized bag. Chloe was coloring a rainbow purple, her broad strokes leaving some stripes dark and some a faint lavender. Tamara smiled down at the drawing, relieved that Chloe was so calm today.

When Dr. Harris opened the door, he introduced himself. "Would you both please come back with me?" he asked with a smile. Chloe looked up at him but sat firm in her chair.

"Come on, baby." Tamara tried to coax her daughter into getting up. "Let's go. It's time to see the doctor."

Chloe looked up at her mother with resistance in her eyes. Tamara saw that Chloe wanted to please her—but she wanted to finish her rainbow even more.

Dr. Harris smiled down at the child. "We have some time," he said, his hazel eyes warm and understanding.

"Thank you," Tamara said. The last thing she wanted was to start their session with Chloe upset.

Dr. Harris took a seat next to Chloe and crossed his right ankle over his left knee. "That's a beautiful rainbow," he said to Chloe. "You like purple."

Chloe looked up and nodded, her face lighting up. "Purple is my favorite color. What's your favorite color?"

Dr. Harris chuckled. "I've always liked blue, I suppose."

Chloe nodded, smiling. "I like blue, too."

"That's good to know. Chloe, I'm going to talk with you and your mom today, but I'd like to see your mom for a few minutes first. Why don't you keep coloring out here while Ms. Matthews watches you?" he asked, smiling at his receptionist. "Your mom and I will just be in the next room."

Chloe nodded, unruffled as usual by Tamara's impending departure, and Tamara walked with Dr. Harris toward his office.

"Thank you for being patient with Chloe," Tamara said. She reached into her bag and pulled out the three-ring binder of information she'd begun compiling for her daughter. Feeling equal bits proud and embarrassed, she handed the binder to Dr. Harris. "I know we already filled out the intake paperwork you sent, and you have background information from Dr. Margolis, but I'm starting to realize that the more information I can offer up front, the better. There's her adoption paperwork, her school reports . . . even vaccination records."

Dr. Harris, flipping through the binder, smiled as they entered his office. "Of course. I've spoken to Dr. Margolis, and that, coupled with the intake paperwork and this folder . . . well, you've done a great job compiling her history. Now, before we begin, I would love to know what your expectations are for this visit so that I can be of greater support."

The question took Tamara aback, but she was pleased by the level of personal attention. "Well, we're here for an evaluation, I suppose, to see if you agree with Dr. Margolis's opinion—which we certainly do. Dr. Margolis has encouraged us to explore our options for treatment, which we understand might include medication. I don't like the idea of medicating Chloe, and neither does my husband, but we're at a point where we're ready to listen to what benefits you think medication would provide, if any." Tamara heard the brittle, pleading edges of her voice.

Dr. Harris smiled. "Thank you. That's helpful. I want you to understand that no one on Chloe's team is a magician—especially me. Even if we do opt to go with medication, nothing that I can give her will make her 'all better.'" Dr. Harris's eyes were intense but kind. "Do you understand?"

"Yes, I understand," Tamara said, though her stomach sank a little. If only it were as simple as a magic pill that could erase all the trauma her little girl had lived through. She thought about all the times she'd gotten coughs or colds as a little girl. Her mother would give her a spoonful of grape medicine, and though Tamara cringed at the bitter aftertaste, she knew it would make her feel better. She knew her mother would fix her. If only it could be as easy for Chloe.

"Great. I'd like to visit with Chloe alone now if that's okay with you."

Tamara nodded. She was beginning to see how these visits followed a pattern.

Dr. Harris's meeting with Chloe didn't last more than fifteen minutes. Soon, Chloe again took her seat in the waiting room, and Tamara returned to Dr. Harris's office.

"So?" Tamara asked, half hopeful and half afraid. "What do you recommend?"

"I agree with Dr. Margolis's assessment and do think that Chloe could benefit from medication," Dr. Harris said. "I suggest starting with a stimulant to help her with her ADHD symptoms. We can then evaluate the effects and go from there."

> *Stimulants* are a type of psychotropic medication that induces temporary improvements in mental and/or physical functions. Stimulants are commonly prescribed for children, adolescents, and adults with attention deficit hyperactivity disorder in order to help them calm and focus. Stimulants work by increasing the levels of the neurotransmitter dopamine in the brain.

Tamara nodded. "What else can you tell me about the stimulant? What changes can we hope to see in her behavior? Are there any side effects?"

"You might see some stomach upset, some sleeplessness," Dr. Harris said. "If Chloe is having trouble sleeping at night, I'll prescribe a gentle sleep aid for her; just call our office for a prescription. There's also the possibility that you'll see an increase in irritability. If this is problematic, please also give my office a call. It might take a couple of tries to find the exact right dosage and medication combination. I think overall, though, you'll see improvement shortly."

> All medications, including over-the-counter medications, have the potential for *side effects*. Working closely with a physician can minimize the chance of having significant side effects. Most medication side effects are mild and occur only during the first few days of starting a new medication or increasing the dose.

"How long will she have to be on medication?" she asked. "I mean, is this a lifetime thing? She'll always need something to help her focus?"

"Our goal is always for that not to be the case," Dr. Harris said. "In the short term, improving Chloe's ability to focus will ideally enhance the effects you see through additional therapy and the in-home services you're receiving."

Tamara nodded, comforted by the fact that Dr. Harris was contradicting her fear of a psychiatrist being a prescription-pad-waving fiend. She saw that to some extent, her worries had been irrational. Dr. Harris wanted the best for Chloe, just like the rest of her care team; he was simply approaching it from his angle of expertise.

"Okay," Tamara said. "I'll need to talk it over with my husband, but I'll take the prescription."

Dr. Harris opened his desk drawer and wrote out his prescription order for Chloe's medication. "Since this is the first time Chloe has taken a stimulant, I'd like to see her back here in two weeks. And remember—while we often have to take a few unexpected turns to find the *best* route, we also have to start the car. That's what we're doing today."

Tamara nodded, but she was slightly unsettled by Dr. Harris's analogy. What did he mean by unexpected turns? She'd researched the potential medications that children with Chloe's diagnoses were given, and the stimulant seemed standard . . . but what if something unexpected *did* happen?

Dr. Harris ripped the paper from his prescription pad, jarring Tamara from her thoughts. He gave her a sympathetic smile. "Remember, too, that her therapy is crucial here. Medication is only a piece of the larger puzzle. And if you haven't already, you should begin looking into special education."

Tamara's head was swimming—she wished Darryl were here. It seemed as though the to-do list for Chloe's wellness kept growing, and each item on its own was overwhelming. She had no clue where to begin when it came to special education. And wasn't it possible that Chloe could get better and continue in a mainstream classroom?

"We're going to work this out for your family," Dr. Harris said, and Tamara noticed that her face felt warm: her anxiety must have been palpable. "While there are no guarantees, I will do my best."

. . .

Darryl had just finally fallen asleep when he felt a little hand on the small of his back.

"Daddy." Chloe's stage whisper broke through his tentative rest, sending his heart racing with adrenaline to face a ghost threat.

For nearly three weeks, ever since Tamara had taken Chloe to see the psychiatrist, Chloe had refused to settle into sleep until well after midnight, whereas she usually started to rub her eyes before eight.

Darryl turned around and glanced at the clock: 1:49. "Baby, it's very late. We all need to get some sleep."

"But I'm not sleepy, Daddy. I want to watch *Care Bears*. I want cuddles," Chloe said, nuzzling her nose against her father's. Darryl pulled the covers back and climbed out of bed. He glanced over at Tamara, whose steady breath made her chest rise and fall. She was exhausted, and Darryl scooped Chloe up in his arms to carry her into the living room. He grabbed a quilt with his free hand and positioned the little girl next to him on the couch, her head resting on his chest as he searched through the DVR for her favorite show.

While the past few weeks at home had been exhausting, Chloe's behavior at school had shown a perplexing blend of improvement and deterioration. She'd been able to focus more on her tasks, disrupting the class less frequently, but it seemed as though her frustration threshold had dipped dramatically. And instead of grumpy words or hiding in a corner when she was upset, Chloe had acted out against another student, and when the student fought back, Chloe ended up with scratch marks up her arm. Darryl signed the incident report, unsure whether her behavior was escalating on its own or whether the medication was making her more violent. Or perhaps she was just exhausted from lack of sleep.

Darryl found the show Chloe had requested, and as the colorful little bears gathered to shoot lights from their bellies, Chloe snuggled against her father's chest. Darryl lowered his face into the little girl's head and smelled the coconut oil that Tamara massaged into Chloe's hair and scalp every other day. Chloe wouldn't sit still long enough for braids or any intricate hairstyle, so the best Tamara had been able to do was keep her hair natural, in six big braids with plastic clips at the end. The smell of coconut reminded Darryl of beach vacations, and he wondered when he and Tamara had last relaxed together and when they all might be able to vacation as a family.

Tomorrow, we'll call Dr. Harris, Darryl thought as his eyelids lowered and his head grew heavier on his daughter's.

...

The next morning, Tamara was confused to find her bed empty. She went into the kitchen to make a pot of coffee and found Darryl and Chloe snuggled on the couch, fast asleep. She smiled at the two, their resemblance striking. Tamara realized that she'd never looked at them together from quite this angle. Jasmine and Darryl had always been obviously related, and Chloe had taken after her mother. The high cheekbones that framed a button nose, full lips that gave way to a beautiful smile—they were all the same features. Tamara's heart soared. *This is what it's like to have a child*, she realized.

While Darryl and Chloe slept, Tamara phoned Dr. Harris. She insisted on holding until he was available, and when he finally picked up, she launched into a summary of the past three weeks, culminating in yesterday's incident report. He agreed that he needed to see Chloe immediately and told Tamara that he would meet them at the office.

"Baby," Tamara whispered, back in the living room. She leaned over Darryl, putting a hand to his cheek. His eyelids opened slowly, and Tamara could see how heavy they were. "We need to take Chloe in to see Dr. Harris."

Darryl's eyes closed, then opened again. "Now?" he whispered back.

Tamara nodded. "I'm sorry."

Darryl groaned. "Go get dressed. I'll try to wake her up slowly."

Tamara leaned in to give her husband a soft peck on the lips before walking back to their room, hoping that while Dr. Harris hadn't promised her a magic pill, there was another combination that would do what he'd promised: help Chloe deal with her symptoms and have more success with the therapy they'd begun.

At his office, Dr. Harris looked thoughtful as Tamara finished an expanded explanation about Chloe's behavior.

"So, the medication hasn't been effective yet," he said.

"No," Tamara said bluntly.

"I wish I had known sooner," Dr. Harris said. "I see you canceled our appointment last week—why was that?"

Tamara prickled, feeling defensive. "It's our first time, Dr. Harris. We don't know what's considered a normal side effect and what isn't."

Dr. Harris smiled, conciliatory. "I understand, and I'm not blaming you."

Placated, Tamara sighed. "I accidentally double booked us last week and scheduled the first day of in-home services for the day of our appointment. I'm so tired . . . Anyway, at the time, it seemed more important to get in-home started."

Dr. Harris nodded. "I understand. Let's try a different approach. The medication that I will prescribe today is also a stimulant, but it works a little differently. In order for her to begin the new medication, we'll need to wean her off the one she's currently taking. That will take a week." He jotted down some numbers and handed them to Tamara. "These are the doses that she'll need, a little lower each day. On Monday, we'll start the new medication, and I'd like to see her back in two weeks."

With most psychotropic medications, it's important to taper off gently, rather than stop abruptly, in order to avoid potentially unpleasant side effects.

"Thank you," Tamara said. "We'll be here, I promise."

"Good," Dr. Harris said. "Remember, as I said before— unexpected turns can happen. Please keep me posted *before* the two-week point if you notice any problematic changes in her behavior."

Tamara nodded, taking the new prescription from Dr. Harris and sticking it in her purse. Her head was clouded, but her resolve was strong. They would get Chloe where she needed to be.

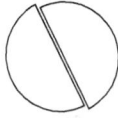

CHAPTER 7

Tamara wasn't sure where they would be if Stacy hadn't known to suggest in-home services. Deidre was the clinical lead, a woman in her thirties with dark auburn hair and whose canvas flats were a dead giveaway of her constant work with children. She led a team of two others, Stephanie and Antonia, whose twenty-something energy was a perfect match for Chloe. The three women had quickly (of course) endeared themselves to Chloe but also to Tamara and Darryl, who had initially been skeptical because of their youth.

Today, Deidre was sitting with Tamara and Darryl in the kitchen for the education component of their program while the others engaged in play therapy with Chloe in the living room. Tamara had bought a dollhouse, and they were working on helping Chloe understand her "circles"—her inner circle being Mommy and Daddy, next circle being teachers and counselors, and so on. Each circle carried different social expectations and boundaries. They were teaching Chloe the differences between how to act at home, at school, and in social settings; whom she could hold hands with and cuddle (her parents); whom she could ask permission for a hug (teachers and counselors); and whom she shouldn't try to ask for permission at all (any unfamiliar adult, even if they were perceived as "safe," such as police officers or firemen). Chloe still struggled, often telling Stephanie and Antonia that she loved them and crawling in their laps without permission, but they gently reminded her about "personal space" and her circles, and some days, Chloe seemed to understand.

"So today I want to talk to you guys about the ARC therapy model," Deidre said. She sat across from them at the kitchen table and slid them some printouts to review. "ARC stands for attachment, self-regulation, and competency, and it's a trauma treatment framework. I'll just go through the four building blocks briefly, since they're things our staff will want to work on with Chloe and with you.

"First, there's consistent response—Mom and Dad, that means you're being consistent in the schedule, in the expectations, and in the response when expectations aren't met and the praise when they are. That's one building block. Another is routines and rituals. Routines are rhythmic; they help us regulate. So we'd like to work on developing a bedtime routine that is regulating, a daytime routine that is regulating. Number three is caregiver affect management."

"What's that?" Tamara interrupted.

"Well, working on all of this is hard. It's challenging for Chloe and challenging for you two, as her caregivers. What are some things you can do to support yourselves? Some of our parents go to support groups, for example. But it's also important to know how to self-regulate *yourselves* in difficult times. If Chloe's having a moment, how will you keep calm enough to provide her with that consistent response we talked about? It's things like that."

Darryl nodded. "Sounds easier said than done sometimes," he said.

Deidre smiled. "Agreed. That's why we talk about it, why we practice. It's not necessarily going to come naturally during tough times."

"What's the fourth building block?" Tamara asked.

"Attunement," Deidre answered. "It's a basic reflective response. Let's say Chloe does something wrong—she's becoming dysregulated, hyper, or she's just thrown a toy or yelled. Our instinct might be to say something like, 'Chloe, knock it off or else!' Especially if we're tired or it's been a long day. But that can contribute to a meltdown. Instead, we want to *reflect* the emotion she's feeling. Let's say she's throwing a tantrum because she can't go outside. We want to say something like, 'Chloe, you seem like you're pretty upset right now. I know we all get kind of upset when we're disappointed, when we can't do what we want to do.' Reflecting and validating her emotions will go a long way toward helping *her* recognize and eventually regulate those same emotions."

Deidre paused. "I know that's a lot," she said with a laugh.

"It is," Tamara said, looking at the printouts Deidre had given them, "but it's good, too. These are the things we wouldn't know to do otherwise."

"Right," Deidre said, nodding. "So the ARC model is really focused on the caregiving system: parents connecting and reflecting emotions, taking care of themselves, being consistent, and having routines and rituals that support regulation."

Darryl looked thoughtfully at Tamara. "It really points out that we're a huge part of this," he said. "We've talked about the things we want to 'fix' in Chloe, but clearly, we need to make our own changes."

"It's a process," Deidre assured them. "These are things we talk about, think about, practice—but it takes time. No one expects you to master all this overnight."

That was something Tamara appreciated about Deidre— she intuitively knew when and how to reassure them.

...

Over the next several months, the work was intensive. Tamara hung up visual schedules in Chloe's room, the kitchen, and the living room, which showed wakeup time, breakfast time, school drop-off time, school pickup time, dinnertime, shower time, and bedtime, along with times that the in-home services team came over or that they had appointments with Drs. Margolis or Harris. It was amazing to Tamara, the comfort this seemed to bring Chloe. She'd look at the clock and say, "Mam—it's almost time for dinner!" Tamara would nod and hug Chloe in praise, telling her she was exactly right and asking whether she'd like to help set the table, which Chloe inexplicably loved.

The new structure had brought unexpected relief for Tamara and Darryl, as well. He was no longer working late in order to be home for dinner, and because Chloe was in bed at eight every night—the effects of the first stimulant a far-flung memory—they had two hours in which to sit on the couch and either talk or watch TV. Even the latter, just sitting side by side, their gaze on the same moving images, made them feel closer.

Stephanie had helped Tamara create a basic behavioral incentive for Chloe. She didn't recommend a point sheet or sticker chart; it was simply a whiteboard with a checkbox beside each morning and evening activity (wake up on time, brush teeth, eat breakfast on time . . .). If Chloe completed the activities successfully, she gleefully marked the box with a dry erase marker. If all her morning boxes were checked off, she got a treat—a small bowl of blueberries or baby carrots, both of which she loved. If her evening boxes were checked off, she got a bubble bath.

This was working so well at home that Deidre had talked with Bianca at school, and they'd implemented a similar system there. Chloe's reward was getting to hug Bianca.

The in-home team talked with the school as well as with Dr. Margolis and Dr. Harris on a regular basis. They wanted to make sure, Deidre explained, that they were all on the same page—that no one was stepping on each other's toes or contradicting each other's treatment plans. As a result, family therapy became a seamless extension of their in-home work.

Once a week, Stephanie or Antonia took Chloe into the community for a social outing. They did simple things that were, at the same time, profound, such as taking Chloe to McDonald's one Saturday. Stephanie prepped Chloe in advance: they were going to a restaurant for lunch, they would order some food, and they would sit next to people they didn't know.

"We don't sit on strangers' laps," Stephanie reminded Chloe before they left. "We sit in the chair by ourselves. We don't stare at people."

Chloe nodded seriously. She was eager to please the adults in her life, even if she sometimes forgot exactly how. That day, she slid beneath the table and started to approach the family one table over. But before she dashed over, she looked at Stephanie, and Stephanie told Tamara later that she could see Chloe's little wheels turning. "We don't go talk to strangers?" Chloe said finally, uncertain.

"No, we don't go talk to strangers," Stephanie said. "Great work, Chloe! Why don't you come back and finish your apple slices?"

...

In one meeting with Dr. Margolis, Tamara asked a question that had been turning over in her mind for weeks.

"Doctor," she said, hesitating, "we've seen some great progress with Chloe over the last few months. I've been wondering, though—what happens to these kids when they're teenagers? When they're adults? I mean, can Chloe fully . . . heal?"

Dr. Margolis gave Tamara a small smile, one that was soothing but not buoyant. "I'll be honest," she said. "There's not a lot of literature about how children with DSED present later in life, which is really unfortunate. But with Chloe's ADHD well controlled with meds, as it seems to be, and the increased social awareness, things can definitely get better. She might always have some problems connecting with others—differentiating between true affection and instinctive attachment—but again, the work you're doing with her gives her more than a fighting chance."

Tamara nodded. It wasn't what she'd wanted to hear, exactly. But it was closer than she'd once thought they'd ever come.

EPILOGUE

Tamara and Darryl were watching a well-worn DVD copy of *The Sound of Music* with Chloe when they noticed that their little girl was sitting in her mini rocking chair holding her baby doll close. Chloe kept casting sidelong glances at her parents, and finally Tamara made eye contact with her. "Are you enjoying the show, Chloe?" she asked.

Chloe nodded and got up to take a seat between her parents. "Do you see how I'm holding Susie?" she asked, showing her mother how she had the baby cuddled into the crook of her arm and close to her chest.

"I do. How nice for baby Susie," Tamara said, smiling.

"It's 'cause I'm her mama. Mamas hold babies like this. This is how mamas hold their babies," Chloe said, scooting closer to her mother.

"It is, baby." Tamara wrapped her arm around the little girl's shoulders.

Everyone had seen a drastic change in Chloe since she'd started the new medication, her therapeutic treatment, and the in-home treatment that she had for five hours a week. At school, Chloe had been able to focus on her tasks and had made tremendous academic gains. She was able to read a short book all on her own, and she was even starting addition. In the family sessions with Dr. Margolis, Chloe was expressing her emotions and needs with more words and staying closer to her parents.

"Mamas and daddies are inner circle, so the baby loves

them most of all. They hold her and feed her," Chloe said proudly. "I'm her mama. And you're my mama." Chloe got even closer to Tamara. "Will you show me how you hold a baby?"

"I'd love to," Tamara replied, watching as Chloe put the baby doll carefully next to Darryl and climbed into her lap. Tamara supported Chloe's neck and patted her bottom, even as the little girl's legs extended onto the couch beyond her mother's grasp.

"The von Trapp children didn't have a mommy until they had Maria," Chloe said, looking at the screen. "She became their mama. Just like you became my mama. Do you think Maria held the babies?" Chloe asked. Suddenly, Tamara realized why Chloe liked the musical so much.

"I do think that she did, if the babies needed to be held. We're never too big to be held by our mamas," Tamara replied softly, touching Chloe's nose with the pad of her index finger.

"Tomorrow, I'll be a big girl," Chloe said. "I go to kinder-garten with the big kids. Will you still rock me?" Chloe's brown eyes looked concerned.

"I'll be your mama every single day for the rest of my life. You'll never get too big for me to rock and love," Ta-mara reassured her daughter, whose eyes were finally more trusting.

As the von Trapps sang goodnight, Tamara knew that it was time to get Chloe ready for bed. "We all have a big day tomorrow," she said to Chloe. "We need to get some sleep."

"Do you think that my teacher will like me?" Chloe asked. She was reluctant to leave Bianca behind.

Darryl had been taking in the scene of his wife and

daughter and couldn't stay quiet any longer. "You just have to use good manners and follow directions, and I think she will like you very much."

Chloe yawned. "I think so, too."

Darryl took Chloe into his arms and carried her to her bed to tuck her in.

"Baby girl, we love you so much," he said, smiling down at her tucked beneath her pink comforter.

"I love you, too, Daddy. Are you going to leave me at the big school in the morning?" she asked, hesitation in her eyes.

"Yes. We'll take you, find your desk, and then we'll go to work. We'll be back to pick you up when school is over, and you'll have so many stories to tell us. We can't wait," Darryl said, smoothing a soft tendril of her hair that had fallen loose from her braids.

Chloe yawned again. "Can't you stay?"

Darryl smiled, warmed by Chloe's request. "This is your adventure, baby girl. We can't stay all day, because then it wouldn't belong to you."

"We're always with you, sweetheart," Tamara added, stepping into the room. She leaned down to kiss Chloe's forehead. "But you're a strong, smart girl. We're confident that you're going to show kindergarten a few things."

Chloe sleepily smiled. "Goodnight."

She rolled over, and before Darryl and Tamara could even leave the room, they heard her inhale and sigh, her little body overcome by sleep. They stood in the doorway for a moment, Chloe's black hair the only thing they could see over the comforter. Their daughter was on the right path, finally.

The three of them were a family.

HOW THESE BOOKS WERE CREATED

The ORP Library of disabilities books is the result of heart-felt collaboration between numerous people: the staff of ORP, including the CEO, executive director, psychologists, clinical coordinators, teachers, and more; the families of children with disabilities served by ORP, including some of the children themselves; and the Round Table Companies (RTC) storytelling team. To create these books, RTC conducted dozens of intensive, intimate interviews over a period of months and performed independent research in order to truthfully and accurately depict the lives of these families. We are grateful to all those who donated their time in support of this message, generously sharing their experience, wisdom, and—most importantly—their stories so that the books will ring true. While each story is fictional and not based on any one family or child, we could not have envisioned the world through their eyes without the access we were so lovingly given. It is our hope that in reading this uniquely personal book, you felt the spirit of everyone who contributed to its creation.

ACKNOWLEDGMENTS

Writing this book would not have been possible without the wisdom, patience, and experience of many generous individuals. In particular, the authors would like to thank retired Genesee Lake School health services director Karen Johnson and Genesee Lake School therapist Christy Lynch for providing valuable information and perspective on the realities and use of psychotropic medication with children. We would also like to thank Kelly Blaschko, director of Genesee Community Services, and Dr. Anne Felden, Genesee Lake School psychologist, for providing real-world examples of treatment plans and therapeutic approaches for community-based services. We also wish to thank Lorri Nelson, ORP executive assistant, for facilitating interviews, organizing material, and generally helping to wrangle the many moving parts that go into writing a book. Finally, we extend a heartfelt thank you to the families who shared their journeys with us in such detail. This group of people was invaluable in bringing Chloe's story to life, and the authors are deeply grateful.

JEFFREY D. KRUKAR, PH.D.

BIOGRAPHY

Jeffrey Krukar, Ph.D., is a licensed psychologist and certified school psychologist with more than 20 years of experience working with children and families in a variety of settings, including community-based group homes, vocational rehabilitation services, residential treatment, juvenile corrections, public schools, and private practice. He earned his Ph.D. in educational psychology, with a school psychology specialization and psychology minor, from the University of Wisconsin-Milwaukee. Dr. Krukar is a Think:Kids Certified Trainer in Collaborative Problem Solving, and an assistant professor at the Wisconsin School of Professional Psychology. He is a registrant of the National Register of Health Service Providers in Psychology, and is also a member of the American Psychological Association.

As the psychologist at Genesee Lake School in Oconomowoc, WI, Dr. Krukar believes it truly takes a village to raise a child—to strengthen developmental foundations in relating, communicating, and thinking—so they can successfully return to their families and communities. Dr. Krukar hopes the ORP Library of disabilities books will bring to light the stories of children and families to a world that is generally not aware of their challenges and successes, as well as offer a sense of hope to those currently on this journey.

KATIE GUTIERREZ

BIOGRAPHY

Katie Gutierrez believes that a well-told story can transcend what a reader "knows" to be real about the world—and thus change the world for that reader. In every form, story is transformative, and Katie is proud to spend her days immersed in it as executive editor for Round Table Companies, Inc.

Since 2007, Katie has edited approximately 50 books and co-written several of the ORP Library of disabilities books, including *Meltdown* and *An Unlikely Trust*. She has been humbled by the stories she has heard and hopes these books will help guide families on their often-lonely journeys, connecting them with resources and support. She also hopes they will give the general population a glimpse into the Herculean jobs taken on so fiercely by parents, doctors, therapists, educators, and others who live with, work with, and love children like Chloe.

Katie holds a BA in English and philosophy from Southwestern University and an MFA in fiction from Texas State University. She has contributed to or been profiled in publications including *Forbes*, *Entrepreneur* magazine, *People* magazine, *Hispanic Executive Quarterly*, and *Narrative* magazine. She can't believe she's lucky enough to do what she loves every day.

CHELSEA McCUTCHIN

BIOGRAPHY

Chelsea McCutchin is a writer, student, teacher, daughter, wife, and mom. When she isn't doing all of the above, you can find her sleeping. Or dreaming. Sometimes at the same time.

NICOLETTE E. WEISENSEL, M.D., F.A.P.A.

BIOGRAPHY

Nicolette E. Weisensel, M.D., F.A.P.A., is a board-certified psychiatrist who has experience in a variety of practice settings including outpatient, inpatient, residential, and day treatment. She has expertise in the treatment of eating disorders and Prader-Willi syndrome. Dr. Weisensel earned her M.D. from the University of Wisconsin School of Medicine and Public Health. She also completed her psychiatry residency at the University of Wisconsin, serving as chief resident during her final year. She has presented at regional, national, and international conferences regarding eating disorders and Prader-Willi syndrome. She is a member and fellow of the American Psychiatric Association.

JAMES G. BALESTRIERI

BIOGRAPHY

James G. Balestrieri is currently the CEO of Oconomowoc Residential Programs, Inc. (ORP). He has worked in the human services field for over 40 years, holding positions that run the gamut to include assistant maintenance, assistant cook, direct care worker, teacher's aide, summer camp counselor, bookkeeper, business administrator, marketing director, CFO, and CEO. Jim graduated from Marquette University with a B.S. in Business Administration (1977) and a Master's in Business Administration with an emphasis in Marketing (1988). He is also a Certified Public Accountant (Wisconsin—1982). Jim has a passion for creatively addressing the needs of those with impairments by managing the inherent stress among funding, programming, and profitability. He believes that those with a disability enjoy rights and protections that were created by the hard-fought efforts of those who came before them; that the Civil Rights movement is not just for minority groups; and that people with disabilities have a right to find their place in the world and to achieve their maximum potential as individuals. For more information, see *www.orp.com*.

ABOUT ORP

Oconomowoc Residential Programs, Inc. is an employee-owned family of companies making a difference in the lives of people with disabilities. With service locations throughout Wisconsin and Indiana, our dedicated staff of 2,400 people provides quality services and professional care to more than 1,950 children, adolescents, and adults with special needs. ORP provides a comprehensive continuum of care. Child and adolescent programs include developmentally appropriate education and treatment in settings specifically attuned to their needs. These include residential therapeutic education and vocational services for students from all around the country. For those in or near Wisconsin and Indiana, we offer community-based residential supports, in-home supports, in- and out-of-home respite care, and alternative therapeutic day school programs. We provide special programs for students with specific academic and social issues relative to a wide range of complex disabilities, including autism spectrum disorders, Asperger's disorder, cognitive and developmental disabilities, anxiety disorders, depression, bipolar disorder, reactive attachment disorder, attention deficit disorder, severe emotional and behavioral issues, Prader-Willi syndrome, and other impairments. Our adult services continuum includes community-based residential services for people with intellectual, developmental, and physical disabilities, brain injury, mental health and other behavioral impairments, and the medically fragile.

We also provide independent living homes, supervised apartments, community-based supports for adults in mental health crisis, day service programs, and respite services.

At ORP, our guiding principle is passion: a passion for the people we serve and for the work we do.

For a comprehensive look at each of our programs, please visit *www.orp.com.* For a collection of resources for parents, educators and administrators, and health-care professionals who are raising or supporting children with disabilities, please visit the ORP Library at *www.orplibrary.com.*

RESOURCES FOR FAMILIES, LOVED ONES, AND PROFESSIONALS

American Academy of Child and Adolescent Psychiatry
www.aacap.org

American Psychiatric Association
www.psychiatry.org

Early Periodic Screening, Diagnosis, and Treatment (EPSDT)
www.mchb.hrsa.gov/epsdt/overview.html

Mayo Clinic
www.mayoclinic.org

National Alliance on Mental Illness (NAMI)
www.nami.org

National Institute of Mental Health
www.nimh.nih.gov

Think:Kids Collaborative Problem Solving
www.thinkkids.org/learn/our-collaborative-problem-solving
-approach

Understanding Mental Disorders: Your Guide to DSM-5

University of Wisconsin Hospital and Clinics
www.uwhealth.org

PSYCHOTROPIC MEDICATIONS

Can I Go Home with You? is the third book in the ORP Library focusing on the use of psychotropic medication in children and adolescents. Based on dozens of interviews with parents and clinicians, this book tells the fictional (but all too real) story of Chloe, a four-year-old diagnosed with disinhibited social engagement disorder as a result of her traumatic past. The book follows *Connecting with Max* and *Finding Balance*, which tell the stories of Max and Alex, respectively. Max is a twelve-year-old diagnosed with autism, and Alex, at seventeen, has been diagnosed with bipolar disorder. All three books explore challenges with side effects, treatment adherence, and dosage and medication changes, as well as highlight successes and explain the importance of a comprehensive biopsychosocial treatment plan. This series aims to educate families, caregivers, and healthcare professionals on the short-term and long-term impact of including psychotropic medication in a child's treatment plan.

FINDING BALANCE
A FAMILY'S JOURNEY TO TREATMENT FOR BIPOLAR DISORDER

CONNECTING WITH MAX
HOW MEDICATION CLOSED THE GAP BETWEEN A FAMILY AND THEIR SON WITH AUTISM

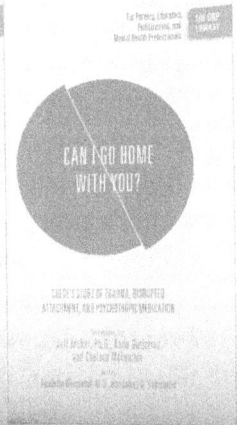

CAN I GO HOME WITH YOU?
CHLOE'S STORY OF TRAUMA, DISRUPTED ATTACHMENT, AND PSYCHOTROPIC MEDICATION

Look for a companion comic book on children and psychotropic medications coming soon!

ASPERGER'S DISORDER

Meltdown and its companion comic book, *Melting Down*, are both based on the fictional story of Benjamin, a boy diagnosed with Asperger's disorder and additional challenging behavior. From the time Benjamin is a toddler, he and his parents know he is different: he doesn't play with his sister, refuses to make eye contact, and doesn't communicate well with others. And his tantrums are not like normal tantrums; they're meltdowns that will eventually make regular schooling—and day-to-day life—impossible. Both the prose book, intended for parents, educators, and mental health professionals, and the comic for the kids themselves demonstrate that the journey toward hope isn't simple . . . but with the right tools and teammates, it's possible.

MELTDOWN

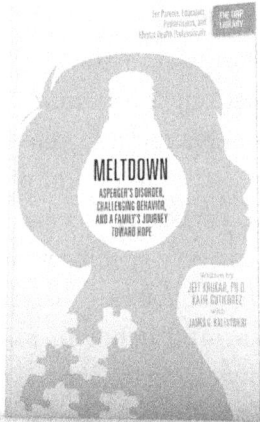

ASPERGER'S DISORDER, CHALLENGING BEHAVIOR, AND A FAMILY'S JOURNEY TOWARD HOPE

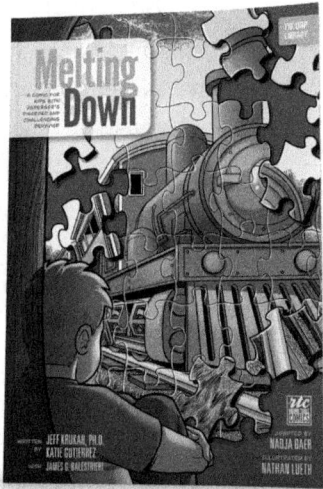

MELTING DOWN

A COMIC FOR KIDS WITH ASPERGER'S DISORDER AND CHALLENGING BEHAVIOR

AUTISM SPECTRUM DISORDER

Mr. Incredible shares the fictional story of Adam, a boy diagnosed with autistic disorder. On Adam's first birthday, his mother recognizes that something is different about him: he recoils from the touch of his family, preferring to accept physical contact only in the cool water of the family's pool. As Adam grows older, he avoids eye contact, is largely nonverbal, and has very specific ways of getting through the day; when those habits are disrupted, intense meltdowns and self-harmful behavior follow. From seeking a diagnosis to advocating for special education services, from keeping Adam safe to discovering his strengths, his family becomes his biggest champion. The journey to realizing Adam's potential isn't easy, but with hope, love, and the right tools and teammates, they find that Adam truly is *Mr. Incredible*. The companion comic in this series, inspired by social stories, offers an innovative, dynamic way to guide children—and parents, educators, and caregivers—through some of the daily struggles experienced by those with autism.

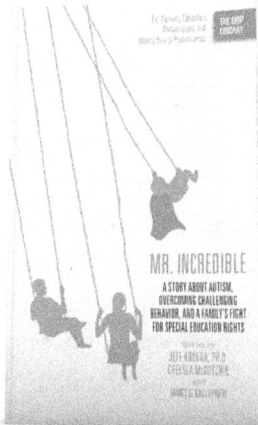

MR. INCREDIBLE

A STORY ABOUT AUTISM,
OVERCOMING CHALLENGING
BEHAVIOR, AND A FAMILY'S FIGHT
FOR SPECIAL EDUCATION RIGHTS

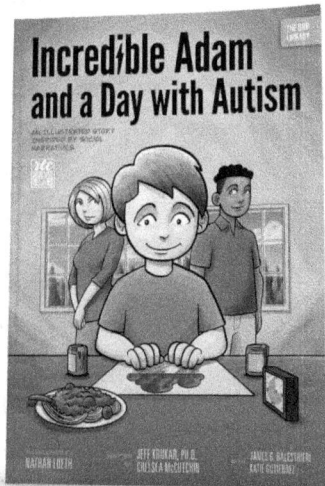

INCREDIBLE ADAM
AND A DAY WITH AUTISM

AN ILLUSTRATED STORY
INSPIRED BY SOCIAL NARRATIVES

BULLYING

Nearly one third of all school children face physical, verbal, social, or cyber bullying on a regular basis. Educators and parents search for ways to end bullying, but as that behavior becomes more sophisticated, it's harder to recognize and stop. In *Classroom Heroes*, Jason is a quiet, socially awkward seventh grader who has long suffered bullying in silence. His parents notice him becoming angrier and more withdrawn, but they don't realize the scope of the problem until one bully takes it too far—and one teacher acts on her determination to stop it. Both *Classroom Heroes* and *How to Be a Hero*—along with a supporting coloring book (*Heroes in the Classroom*) and curriculum guide (*Those Who Bully and Those Who Are Bullied*)—recognize that stopping bullying requires a change in mindset: adults and children must create a community that simply does not tolerate bullying. These books provide practical yet very effective strategies to end bullying, one student at a time.

CLASSROOM HEROES

ONE CHILD'S STRUGGLE WITH BULLYING AND A TEACHER'S MISSION TO CHANGE SCHOOL CULTURE

HOW TO BE A HERO

A COMIC BOOK ABOUT BULLYING

HEROES IN THE CLASSROOM

AN ACTIVITY BOOK ABOUT BULLYING

THOSE WHO BULLY AND THOSE WHO ARE BULLLIED

A GUIDE FOR CREATING HEROES IN THE CLASSROOM

FAMILY SUPPORT

Schuyler Walker was just four years old when he was diagnosed with autism, bipolar disorder, and ADHD. In 2004, childhood mental illness was rarely talked about or understood. With knowledge and resources scarce, Schuyler's mom, Christine, navigated a lonely maze to determine what treatments, medications, and therapies could benefit her son. In the years since his diagnosis, Christine has often wished she had a "how to" guide that would provide the real mom-to-mom information she needed to survive the day and, in the end, help her family navigate the maze with knowledge, humor, grace, and love. Christine may not have had a manual at the beginning of her journey, but she hopes this book will serve as yours.

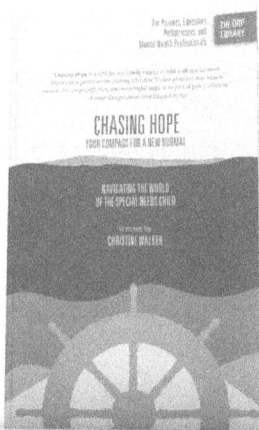

CHASING HOPE
YOUR COMPASS FOR A NEW NORMAL

NAVIGATING THE WORLD
OF THE SPECIAL NEEDS CHILD

PRADER-WILLI SYNDROME

Estimated to occur once in every 15,000 births, Prader-Willi syndrome is a rare genetic disorder that includes features of cognitive disabilities, problem behaviors, and, most pervasively, chronic hunger that leads to dangerous overeating and its life-threatening consequences. *Insatiable: A Prader-Willi Story* and its companion comic book, *Ultra-Violet: One Girl's Prader-Willi Story*, draw on dozens of intensive interviews to offer insight into the world of those struggling with Prader-Willi syndrome. Both books tell the fictional story of Violet, a vivacious young girl born with the disorder, and her family, who—with the help of experts—will not give up their quest to give her a healthy and happy life.

INSATIABLE
A PRADER-WILLI STORY

ULTRA-VIOLET
ONE GIRL'S PRADER-WILLI STORY

REACTIVE ATTACHMENT DISORDER

Loving Harder, *An Unlikely Trust*, and *Alina's Story* share the journeys of children diagnosed with reactive attachment disorder. *Loving Harder* is the true story of the Hetzel family, while *An Unlikely Trust* is a composite story based on dozens of intensive interviews with parents and clinicians. *Alina's Story* is a companion children's book and valuable therapeutic tool, offering a beautiful and accessible way for children with RAD to understand their own stories. The families in these books know their adopted children need help and work endlessly to find it, eventually discovering a special school that will teach the children new skills. Slowly, the children get better at expressing their feelings and solving problems. For the first time in their lives, they realize they are safe and loved . . . and capable of loving in return.

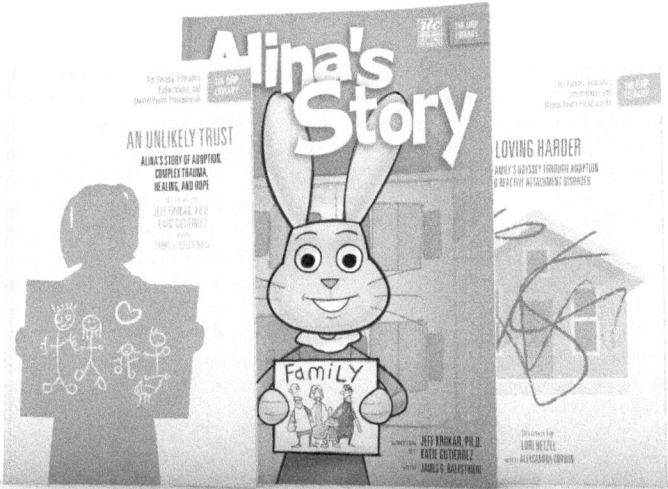

AN UNLIKELY TRUST
ALINA'S STORY OF ADOPTION, COMPLEX TRAUMA, HEALING, AND HOPE

ALINA'S STORY
LEARNING HOW TO TRUST, HEAL, AND HOPE

LOVING HARDER
OUR FAMILY'S ODYSSEY THROUGH ADOPTION AND REACTIVE ATTACHMENT DISORDER

www.ingramcontent.com/pod-product-compliance
Lightning Source LLC
La Vergne TN
LVHW051134080426
835510LV00018B/2406